T0316246

PROVING MR JENNINGS

James Walker

PROVING MR JENNINGS

OBERON BOOKS
LONDON

WWW.OBERONBOOKS.COM

First published in 2007 by Oberon Books Ltd.
521 Caledonian Road, London N7 9RH
Tel: 020 7607 3637 / Fax: 020 7607 3629
e-mail: info@oberonbooks.com
www.oberonbooks.com

A catalogue record for this book is available from the British
Library.

PB ISBN: 978-1-84002-719-8

Cover design by Andrzej Klimowski

Visit www.oberonbooks.com to read more about all our books
and to buy them. You will also find features, author interviews and
news of any author events, and you can sign up for e-newsletters
so that you're always first to hear about our new releases.

Characters

in order of appearance

NURSE DAVIDS
early twenties

CHARLES JENNINGS
mid/late forties

MR GIBBONS
fifties

AGENT PSMITH
late twenties to late thirties

COLONEL LOVEDAY
forties

SYLVIE JENNINGS
late thirties/early forties

Proving Mr Jennings was first produced at the Courtyard Theatre, London in 2004, with the following cast:

CHARLES JENNINGS Daniel Hill

NURSE DAVIDS Gemma Saunders

MR GIBBONS Christopher Naylor

AGENT PSMITH Paul Vaughan Evans

COLONEL LOVEDAY Tim Frances

SYLVIE JENNINGS Lucy Scott

Directed by Guy Retallack

ACT ONE

Scene 1

Lights up on a hospital room. Watery sunshine from the early afternoon filters in from a high window. A distant murmur of traffic. In the centre of the room, a vacant bed is stripped of linen. Beside it, a locker; an alarm clock. A changing screen stands, upright and folded, beside the bed. A generous vase of red roses perches on a table beside a chair. A door leads off. Footsteps and voices, off. A young woman enters briskly.

NURSE DAVIDS: (*Expansively.*) Here we are!

> *NURSE DAVIDS is pretty, in her early twenties, with a lively spring in her step. Her energy is captivating, the skittishness adding to her allure. She carries a small parcel of sheets.*

(*With enthusiasm.*) The Penthouse Suite!

> *She is followed into the room by CHARLES JENNINGS. In his mid-forties, JENNINGS is still in good shape. He wears a traditional overcoat and beneath, a tailored suit. He is carrying a small overnight case. Careful with his words and precise in his movements, JENNINGS surveys the room.*

JENNINGS: Splendid. Charming. Very charming indeed.

NURSE DAVIDS: (*Crossing to the window.*) We're well situated here. South facing. Smashing view of the river.

JENNINGS: (*Peering out.*) Delightful.

NURSE DAVIDS: It's a teeny-weeny bit dark in the mornings, but in summer this is a *very* popular room.

JENNINGS: I dare say.

> *NURSE DAVIDS motions towards the vase.*

NURSE DAVIDS: I bought you some flowers, look. Can be a bit drab on the wards. I thought they might…perk things up a bit.

JENNINGS: How terribly kind of you.

NURSE DAVIDS: I asked for twenty-one exactly.

JENNINGS: (*No expert on flora.*) Roses…

NURSE DAVIDS: One for every year.

JENNINGS: You shouldn't have gone to any trouble.

NURSE DAVIDS: It was my birthday yesterday. (*Unnecessarily.*) I'm twenty-one.

JENNINGS: (*Awkwardly.*) My wife's favourites, roses.

Uncomfortable pause.

They both begin at the same time.

NURSE DAVIDS: (*Overlapping.*) Would you like me –

JENNINGS: (*Overlapping.*) It's a cracking –

Pause.

JENNINGS: Thank you. Just the ticket.

NURSE DAVIDS: You can take your coat off now, Mr…?

JENNINGS: Jennings. Charles Jennings.

NURSE DAVIDS: (*Holding out her hand.*) Nurse Davids.

JENNINGS: (*Shaking it.*) Pleased to meet you.

She takes his coat from him.

NURSE DAVIDS: Did you bring a gown?

JENNINGS: A dressing gown?

NURSE DAVIDS: Something to wear in theatre.

JENNINGS: I thought that might be supplied.

NURSE DAVIDS: Back in a jiffy.

She exits with his coat, flashing a smile as she goes.

JENNINGS settles in; gets a feel for the place.

He runs his finger along the bedside table. Wincing, he wipes a veneer of dust from the table. He searches for a place to dispose of it subtly. He takes a medical bleeper from his belt and lays it safely down on the bedside locker. Opening his case, he discovers a card. He puts on his reading glasses and admires it fondly.

NURSE DAVIDS re-enters silently, carrying a clipboard. She observes him.

Can I help you with anything?

JENNINGS: (*Touched.*) No, no – just Harry – my boy – he's made me a 'Get Well' card.

NURSE DAVIDS moves over to have a look. The card is daubed in lurid crayon.

(*Pointing out a figure, proudly.*) It's a picture of our house. That's my wife.

NURSE DAVIDS: (*Brightly.*) She's enormous, isn't she?

JENNINGS: It's not to scale.

NURSE DAVIDS: Mind if I hang on to it? (*Tucking it into her clipboard.*) For safety.

JENNINGS: (*Reluctantly.*) I had hoped –

NURSE DAVIDS: Why don't you get yourself ready?

JENNINGS: Where did you put my coat?

NURSE DAVIDS: You worry about getting that gown on.

JENNINGS: I don't have a gown. You were kindly going to fetch me one.

NURSE DAVIDS: (*Puzzled.*) I was?

JENNINGS: That was my impression.

NURSE DAVIDS: What's wrong with the one you've got?

JENNINGS: (*Patiently.*) I don't have one.

NURSE DAVIDS: What's this, then?

She pulls back the pillow with a flourish and conjures a hospital gown.

JENNINGS: How kind.

NURSE DAVIDS: You'd like me to get into bed?

JENNINGS: Excuse me?

NURSE DAVIDS: You'd like me to set the bed?

JENNINGS: Yes. Right. Splendid.

NURSE DAVIDS: Feeling alright?

JENNINGS: Remarkably well – all things considered.

NURSE DAVIDS: Everything okay so far?

JENNINGS: First-rate.

NURSE DAVIDS: Smashing.

NURSE DAVIDS billows out the sheets. She makes the bed, bending ostentatiously as she does so.

Gorgeous room this. I've had some times in this room.

JENNINGS: (*Stiffly.*) I expect the surgeon will want to drop by later. Touch base, that sort of thing. Lengthy procedure, I understand.

NURSE DAVIDS: (*Bouncing the bed up and down.*) Look at the springs on that!

JENNINGS: Only I'd like to give him something.

NURSE DAVIDS: Who?

JENNINGS: The surgeon.

NURSE DAVIDS: I'm not your type?

JENNINGS: (*Embarrassed.*) No…not at all…what I meant was…I'd like to buy him something and I wondered…well, I thought it might be nice… (*He tails off.*)

An awkward pause.

I'll be back shortly.

JENNINGS pivots for the door.

NURSE DAVIDS skips nimbly round to block it.

NURSE DAVIDS: (*Firmly.*) You can't leave.

JENNINGS: Why not?

NURSE DAVIDS: Doctor's orders.

JENNINGS goes for the door handle.

NURSE DAVIDS sways so that his hand is intercepted by her waist. Her body language is predatory.

JENNINGS: (*Muttering.*) There's bound to be somewhere close by I could pick something up –

NURSE DAVIDS: I've always had a thing for older patients.

JENNINGS: Yes, well I think it would be bad form –

NURSE DAVIDS: I'm not going to bite…

NURSE DAVIDS advances.

JENNINGS retreats into the room.

JENNINGS: Not to show…a token of my…gratitude.

NURSE DAVIDS: (*Holding out the hospital robe.*) Why don't you slip into something a little more comfortable?

JENNINGS: (*Confused.*) Thank you.

JENNINGS inspects the gown.

NURSE DAVIDS consults her checklist.

NURSE DAVIDS: You took those tablets?

JENNINGS: (*Distracted.*) Sorry?

NURSE DAVIDS: The tablets?

JENNINGS: What tablets?

NURSE DAVIDS: The ones I gave you.

JENNINGS: I don't recall any –

NURSE DAVIDS: What was your name again?

JENNINGS: Jennings. Charles Jennings.

NURSE DAVIDS: (*Looking hard at him.*) I've seen your face before.

JENNINGS: No. I don't think so.

NURSE DAVIDS: You've been on television –

JENNINGS: (*Concerned.*) Are they important?

NURSE DAVIDS: I'm sure I've seen you somewhere…

JENNINGS: Are they important?

NURSE DAVIDS: Who?

JENNINGS: The tablets.

   Pause.

NURSE DAVIDS: (*Vacantly.*) Tablets?

JENNINGS: You asked me just now if I'd taken some tablets.

NURSE DAVIDS: Would you *like* to take a tablet?

JENNINGS: (*Beginning to lose patience.*) Is it *necessary*?

NURSE DAVIDS: For what?

JENNINGS: My health.

NURSE DAVIDS: Depends which tablet you take. There are hundreds of tablets I could give you. Which one do you want?

JENNINGS: I hoped you might tell me. I thought that's how thing's worked in a hospital.

NURSE DAVIDS: If you've lost medication, Mr…

JENNINGS: (*Helping her.*) Jennings –

NURSE DAVIDS: (*Defensively.*) I'm afraid it's no use trying to palm the blame off onto the nursing staff!

JENNINGS scrutinises the robe.

JENNINGS: What is that?

NURSE DAVIDS: What?

JENNINGS: (*Pointing at the front of the robe.*) That.

She inspects.

NURSE DAVIDS: Where?

JENNINGS: There. It looks like a stain.

She takes a closer look. There's a dark aureole of filth daubed across the front.

NURSE DAVIDS: Call that a stain?

JENNINGS: This has been washed?

She sniffs it.

NURSE DAVIDS: Should think so.

JENNINGS: I'd prefer a new one, if you don't mind. There are limits to the term 'Public Health'.

NURSE DAVIDS: Would you like to lodge a formal complaint?

JENNINGS: (*With restraint.*) I'm starting to consider it.

NURSE DAVIDS: Or would you rather have a tablet?

JENNINGS: I would like to do whatever it is I am *required* to do, Nurse Davids. I would like to feel secure in your care – reassured by a childlike sense that you have everything in hand. And whilst I recognise that in your profession a little improvisation is *de rigueur*, I cannot stifle the notion that you may be operating... extempore.

NURSE DAVIDS: Thanks very much!

JENNINGS: That is not a compliment.

NURSE DAVIDS: (*Disappointed.*) Oh.

JENNINGS: Are you qualified?

NURSE DAVIDS: Practically.

JENNINGS: A trainee?

NURSE DAVIDS: It's an arduous career. Can take months to apply.

JENNINGS: (*Stunned.*) I'm admitted to hospital for a life-saving operation and the best the NHS can offer me is an impending learner?

NURSE DAVIDS: You should see me in a négligé.

JENNINGS: (*Stopped in his tracks.*) What was that?

NURSE DAVIDS: (*Quick.*) Sounds like you're accusing me of negligence.

JENNINGS: Far from it, my girl. In fact, as a lawyer, I'm choosing my words very carefully.

NURSE DAVIDS: I'm picking it up very fast, actually.

JENNINGS: (*Indicating the robe.*) You were evidently indisposed the day they covered hygiene.

NURSE DAVIDS: Looks all right to me.

JENNINGS: It does?

NURSE DAVIDS: Fresh as a daisy!

JENNINGS: Then I cannot help but arrive at one of the following conclusions: either your knowledge of flora is startlingly perverse, or I shall assume you served your last apprenticeship in an abattoir.

Pause.

NURSE DAVIDS: This is a flagship hospital.

JENNINGS: I realise that, Miss Davids.

NURSE DAVIDS: *Nurse* Davids.

JENNINGS: As I say.

NURSE DAVIDS: We're up for Foundation status!

JENNINGS: This garment is a disgrace!

NURSE DAVIDS: I probably shouldn't be telling you this, Mr...

JENNINGS: *Jennings*!

NURSE DAVIDS: (*To herself.*) *Jennings, Jennings...* (*Gathering herself.*) But if you could see the kind of hothouses passed off as hospitals in the rest of the country: patients squatting openly in the corridors, nurses in waders sloshing through puddles; kitchens alive with mice and weevils; infected air skipping freely from one ward to the next; great footballs of dust clogging up the ventilation shafts; syringes handed willy-nilly from patient to patient without so much as a wipe with a wet Kleenex!

JENNINGS: You have a vivid imagination, young lady.

NURSE DAVIDS: (*Getting into her stride.*) When I first arrived at this hospital, things weren't so different.

JENNINGS: (*A principle at stake.*) Am I, or am I not, entitled to a clean robe?

NURSE DAVIDS: A lot's changed since then.

JENNINGS: Since when?

NURSE DAVIDS: Since I started here.

JENNINGS: And when was that?

NURSE DAVIDS: Two weeks ago. And already there's a pride about this hospital. So if you're planning to upset things –

JENNINGS: Two weeks!

NURSE DAVIDS: Because between you and I... (*Her tone becomes conspiratorial.*) ...you're very lucky to be seen so quickly.

JENNINGS: (*On thin ice.*) I'm not disputing –

NURSE DAVIDS: Some people have to wait years. My father died waiting for an operation like the one you're having!

JENNINGS: (*Genuinely.*) I'm sorry to hear that.

NURSE DAVIDS: I bet you are.

NURSE DAVIDS is flushed.

JENNINGS senses he may have pushed her too far.

JENNINGS: You think this is clean, then?

NURSE DAVIDS: I've got half a mind to cancel this operation.

JENNINGS: (*Backtracking.*) If you tell me it's clean, I'm prepared to take your word for it –

NURSE DAVIDS: I could send you home right now!

JENNINGS: I'm sorry about your father.

NURSE DAVIDS: They're queuing up out there for a new organ!

JENNINGS: If there are any tablets I should take, I'd be happy to –

NURSE DAVIDS: So if you're going to be difficult –

JENNINGS: (*Humility itself.*) Not at all…

NURSE DAVIDS: We're very tight on resources. We have to prioritise.

JENNINGS: I understand that, I really do.

NURSE DAVIDS: Do you? Really?

JENNINGS: I'd be more than happy to put this robe on.

NURSE DAVIDS: Would you now?

JENNINGS: If that's all right with you?

A pause. Finally…

NURSE DAVIDS: Chop chop.

She unfolds the changing screen and ushers JENNINGS one side of the bed to achieve a split-screen effect: the bed and JENNINGS are one side, the chair and NURSE DAVIDS the other.

JENNINGS: Are these the pills you mentioned?

JENNINGS moves round the screen and offers the tablets he's found beside the vase.

NURSE DAVIDS: (*Delighted.*) There they are!

JENNINGS: Should I take one?

NURSE DAVIDS looks him up and down.

NURSE DAVIDS: Do you need it?

JENNINGS: I'm not sure.

NURSE DAVIDS: Try without it first. You might surprise yourself.

JENNINGS observes her intensely for a moment.

NURSE DAVIDS draws the curtain across again. She sits and applies lipstick using a pocket mirror.

JENNINGS begins to change. Something has struck him.

JENNINGS: Do you have a sister, Nurse?

NURSE DAVIDS: Sister?

JENNINGS: Cousin, maybe? Blond girl: freckles, curly hair. Attractive.

NURSE DAVIDS: Lisa?

JENNINGS: (*To himself.*) Lisa…

NURSE DAVIDS: (*Suddenly excited.*) You know Lise!

JENNINGS: You're right – there is something familiar –

NURSE DAVIDS: You're the father!

JENNINGS: What?

NURSE DAVIDS: Gary!

JENNINGS: (*Drawing a blank.*) No, no, I'm – I'm getting confused. I only… No, I don't know your cousin at all.

NURSE DAVIDS: Haven't seen Lise in ages.

He continues to change.

JENNINGS: (*Quietly dawning.*) Gary…hold on a minute… Gary!

NURSE DAVIDS: Can I help you with anything?

JENNINGS scents the trail.

JENNINGS: Does the name 'Gary Bates' mean anything to you?

NURSE DAVIDS: (*Trying it for size.*) Bates…

JENNINGS: Where were you last summer?

NURSE DAVIDS: Last summer?

JENNINGS: Yes – August?

NURSE DAVIDS: Corfu.

JENNINGS: You're sure about that?

NURSE DAVIDS: Fairly sure.

JENNINGS: You weren't in court?

NURSE DAVIDS: Where?

JENNINGS: Wood Green Crown Court.

NURSE DAVIDS: Never been to court –

JENNINGS: With your cousin –

NURSE DAVIDS: (*Genuinely.*) Don't remember –

JENNINGS: (*The details returning.*) Of course…

NURSE DAVIDS: Rings a bell, though –

JENNINGS: I remember the voice…the tattoo!

NURSE DAVIDS feels her bosom instinctively.

JENNINGS draws back the curtain with a flourish.

You recognise me, Nurse Davids, because I prosecuted you.

Dressed in the hospital robe, his appearance jars with the seriousness of the revelation. A beat.

NURSE DAVIDS: (*Hopefully.*) Everything okay?

JENNINGS: 'Okay'?

NURSE DAVIDS: Yes.

JENNINGS: You put me in an impossible position, young lady.

NURSE DAVIDS: (*Bright.*) No position's impossible if you warm up beforehand!

JENNINGS: I arrive for a supposedly life-saving operation at a respected national hospital to find that the hygiene levels compare unfavourably with Mother Teresa's worst nightmare. Moreover, the nurse I am allocated – that is *you*, Nurse Davids – a misleading title I discover – boasts only the rudiments of medical know-how and a string of convictions for fashionable sexual offences. That an amnesiac nymphomaniac should occupy a position of responsibility within the public sector *beggars belief* –

NURSE DAVIDS: They told me I was uniquely qualified.

JENNINGS: (*Bitingly.*) *Did* they?

NURSE DAVIDS: (*Interrupting.*) I thought we could warm up with a relaxing cardiac massage. Then maybe you could take a tablet –

JENNINGS: (*Turning on her.*) Miss Davids! If I am to have one shred of belief in the story of your rehabilitation –

NURSE DAVIDS: (*Popping out two tablets.*) It's quite a kick if we *both* take one –

JENNINGS: I don't believe you have the slightest idea what's in those tablets! They could wreak havoc with my blood pressure for all you know!

NURSE DAVIDS: Exactly!

JENNINGS: Given your criminal past, I am beginning to feel vulnerable!

A moment.

NURSE DAVIDS gathers herself.

NURSE DAVIDS: I appreciate your comments, Mr –

JENNINGS: JENNINGS. J-E-double N-I-N-G-S.

NURSE DAVIDS takes up her clipboard.

NURSE DAVIDS: But before the operation can proceed I have to run through a few routine questions.

JENNINGS: Did you say 'proceed'?

NURSE DAVIDS: (*Helpfully.*) Continue.

JENNINGS: Yes, I understand the word –

NURSE DAVIDS: We have to be sure that the limited organs we have available go to our most deserving clients.

JENNINGS: I thought there was one waiting for me.

NURSE DAVIDS: There is a queue.

JENNINGS: You mean I have to pass some sort of test?

NURSE DAVIDS: Not officially.

JENNINGS: I assumed it was all confirmed –

NURSE DAVIDS: Open!

A reflex more than anything, JENNINGS opens his mouth.

NURSE DAVIDS slots in a thermometer. She reads from her notes.

(*Schoolmistress tone.*) Are you a smoker?

JENNINGS: (*Taking the thermometer out.*) Look, this won't affect whether I get the operation, will it? It's not going to mean you won't treat me?

NURSE DAVIDS: May I remind you: as a man of the law, you are on oath.

She pushes the thermometer back in.

Have you ever smoked a cigarette? Yes or no?

He pauses. Then shakes his head.

Would you ever consider smoking a cigarette in the future?

JENNINGS: (*The thermometer still in.*) Look, it's rather ridiculous if I have to justify –

NURSE DAVIDS: Any childhood illnesses?

JENNINGS: A little asthma. As a boy.

NURSE DAVIDS: Up to date with your vaccinations?

JENNINGS: (*Affirmative.*) Umhuh.

NURSE DAVIDS: Tetanus booster?

JENNINGS: Last year. (*Helpfully.*) June.

She removes the thermometer and takes a reading.

NURSE DAVIDS: Do you seek to enter this hospital to engage in subversive activities?

JENNINGS: (*Nonplussed.*) I beg your pardon?

NURSE DAVIDS: Any allergies that you're aware of?

JENNINGS: No.

NURSE DAVIDS: Previous operations?

JENNINGS: No.

NURSE DAVIDS: Specialist weapons training?

JENNINGS: What?

NURSE DAVIDS: (*Ticking a box and pressing on.*) You're confirmed, I presume?

JENNINGS: Does it matter?

NURSE DAVIDS: Not if you take regular exercise.

JENNINGS: I do.

NURSE DAVIDS: You have a sportsman's behind.

JENNINGS: Thank you.

NURSE DAVIDS: Any history of heart disease in your family?

JENNINGS: On my mother's side.

NURSE DAVIDS: Smashing. Are you a member of any banned organisations?

JENNINGS: Am I a member of what?

NURSE DAVIDS: (*Firmly.*) 'Yes' or 'No'.

JENNINGS: I'm a lifelong member of the MCC but I'm not sure that's going to help you.

NURSE DAVIDS: The which?

JENNINGS: (*Flippantly.*) The Marylebone Cricket Club.

NURSE DAVIDS: (*Making a note.*) Aha.

JENNINGS: You can't seriously be taking that down?

NURSE DAVIDS: You're welcome to join the back of the queue. Any history of high blood pressure?

JENNINGS: On my mother's side – yes.

NURSE DAVIDS: Game?

JENNINGS: Excuse me?

NURSE DAVIDS: Do you eat 'game'?

JENNINGS: Oh. I see. No.

NURSE DAVIDS: Ever participated in genocide?

JENNINGS: (*Flippantly.*) Not lately.

NURSE DAVIDS: (*Straight.*) Fab.

NURSE DAVIDS turns a page.

JENNINGS is bemused.

Would you sign here for me, please?

JENNINGS: That's it? You mean the operation's going to go ahead?

NURSE DAVIDS: Nine o'clock tomorrow morning.

JENNINGS: (*Relieved.*) Splendid!

He signs with a flurry.

NURSE DAVIDS: T'rific!

NURSE DAVIDS folds the form and tucks it discreetly into her pocket. She hangs the clipboard on the end of the bed.

JENNINGS: Any idea when I might be…heading home, as it were? What sort of recovery period we're looking at for an operation like this? A week? Two weeks?

NURSE DAVIDS: Fingers crossed, you'll be out in a flash.

An unwieldy pause.

JENNINGS: So…what happens now?

NURSE DAVIDS: (*Consulting her watch.*) We do have a lot of hours to kill, don't we?

JENNINGS: (*Delving into his case.*) I brought some board games with me.

NURSE DAVIDS: What about…

JENNINGS: Yes?

NURSE DAVIDS: (*Unscrewing the lid, with a twinkle.*) Why don't we both have a tablet and see what happens?

A beat.

Blackout.

Scene 2

A similar room.

Complete silence, save the delicate timbre of JENNINGS' snore.

JENNINGS is lying in the bed, face up and asleep. He is hooked up to a drip. The roses have disappeared (as have JENNINGS' case and clothes) but the alarm clock still squats on the bedside locker. There's an extra grey blanket on the bed. The light is colder.

MR GIBBONS stands over him. In his fifties, distinguished-looking, with a thoughtful, implacable manner, GIBBONS is the kind of man we implicitly trust. He is dressed in the white coat of his profession. He prepares a syringe of clear liquid, which he proceeds to inject into JENNINGS' exposed forearm. He is making a note on his clipboard and consulting his watch when JENNINGS lets out a wail, simultaneously catapulting himself upright in bed.

JENNINGS: WAAH!

> *JENNINGS takes a moment to come to. He casts wild eyes about the room.*

> (*Hazy.*) Where am I?

GIBBONS: You're all right, Mr Jennings. You're in safe hands.

JENNINGS: Who…who are you?

GIBBONS: My name is Mr Gibbons. I'm the surgeon.

JENNINGS: …where am I?

GIBBONS: You're in the hospital.

JENNINGS: How long…how long have I been here?

GIBBONS: We thought it was about time we woke you.

> *JENNINGS rocks back in the bed, sighing. His semi-slumber makes him lucid.*

> How are you feeling?

JENNINGS: Terribly woozy…thirsty…

GIBBONS: You'll soon pick up.

GIBBONS hands him a glass of water.

JENNINGS drinks appreciatively.

JENNINGS: I had the most dreadful nightmare, doctor.

GIBBONS: I'm sorry to hear that.

JENNINGS: So vivid…

GIBBONS: How many fingers am I holding up?

JENNINGS: Three. It was terribly disturbing.

GIBBONS: Look at me, please.

GIBBONS shines a light into his eyes.

Blink. Blink. Fine.

He jots a note.

JENNINGS: I can't get it out of my mind –

GIBBONS: What is your wife's name?

JENNINGS: Sylvie.

GIBBONS: Good.

JENNINGS: My nightmare –

GIBBONS: Would it help to get it off your chest?

JENNINGS: Would you mind?

GIBBONS: (*Looking at his watch, a moment.*) Not at all. Fire away.

JENNINGS is sweating.

JENNINGS: There was a man…in my nightmare…the most
dreadful man…an Arab-looking fellow. He came at me in
the pitch darkness with a pair of shears…garden shears they
were…wrapped in various oriental fabrics, but I knew well
enough what he was after. He…he tied me down and started
prodding and jabbing with his shears in my stomach, forcing
them deeper and deeper until he came up under the rib

cage. He laughed the most horrible laugh, like bells clanging inside my head, and at the same time he opened the shears like great jaws and all I could see was his face – stretched in long lines of mirth – and a curtain pulled all around me…

GIBBONS: (*Gripped.*) And?

JENNINGS: Nothing. I woke up.

GIBBONS: Ah.

JENNINGS: Must have been something I saw on television.

GIBBONS: (*Making notes.*) No need to worry. It's quite usual to dream vividly as the effects of the anaesthetic wear off. (*With interest.*) You're quite sure it was an Arab?

JENNINGS: Your sort of build. But darker, certainly. Arab-looking.

GIBBONS makes a note.

I'm sorry – did you say you were the surgeon?

GIBBONS: Mr Gibbons, yes.

JENNINGS: I can't feel my legs –

GIBBONS: You're still recovering from the effect of the drugs, Mr Jennings. They're liable to make you volatile.

JENNINGS: What day is it?

GIBBONS: Everything's under control. You'll start to feel better as the anaesthetic wears off. However, there's a lot to get through and I don't want to take up any of your precious time. I appreciate you'll be anxious to know how the thing went –

JENNINGS: The anaesthetic… (*Slowly comprehending the momentousness of the thing.*) …of course…the operation! It's done, isn't it? The operation's over?

GIBBONS: That's correct.

JENNINGS: Finished!

GIBBONS: Yes.

JENNINGS: Triumphant! (*A beat.*) Oh, I know! I'm not out of the woods yet. I've fought too many cases of negligence on the part of surgeons not to realise it would be foolish to jump to conclusions. But quite honestly… I feel…renewed! (*Laughing.*) The scales have fallen from my eyes!

GIBBONS: Indeed.

JENNINGS: (*The excitement of life unfolding.*) Between you and I, I had grave doubts about the whole business. But now! A new lease of life! A reprieve! I can feel my heart beating in my chest again! (*Looking at his veins.*) I can actually see the blood rushing through my veins! Look!

GIBBONS: Yes…yes.

JENNINGS: (*Swimming with dreams.*) Restored – that's what I am! Repaired! Healthy! Whole again! Do you know what I'm going to do, Doctor? My resolution? I'm going to live – from this moment on – really live! Not just survive. Up at dawn – the crisp autumn leaves under my feet! I'm going to listen, actually *listen* to the leaves crackling under my feet! I'll take my wife to Venice! I'll let melancholy ripple over us on the Bridge of Sighs! I'll take snapshots of the Taj Mahal at dawn! Drive my boys down Route 66 in a beaten-up old Mustang… Hell! I'll –

GIBBONS: If I may stop you there, Mr Jennings –

JENNINGS: (*Breathless.*) From now on, I won't let a single day slip by without blessing it with an act of the most profound vitality! This is the alarum I've been waiting for! This is the call to arms, Doctor!

GIBBONS: (*Concerned.*) The what?

JENNINGS: The call to arms! The wake-up call! This is the new beginning!

GIBBONS jots a note.

(*Unstoppable.*) Do you understand the momentousness of this moment, Doctor?

GIBBONS: Mr Jennings, there's something I need to discuss with you –

JENNINGS: For the first time since my youth, I feel truly alive!

GIBBONS: Yes, of course – however –

JENNINGS: (*Oblivious in his rapture.*) Oh I know that for reasons of legality you can't divulge the identity of the person whose… (*Correcting himself.*) – sorry, saint – whose heart I carry within me thanks to you – thanks to you both. Oh, the wonders of modern science! You! You, Doctor, with your teams of dedicated back-up staff and nurses – who aren't back-up at all! No – they've got the right to be appreciated for the angels they are! You all, collectively, you the National Health Service are responsible for the miracle that I carry inside me NOW!

GIBBONS: Mr Jennings, we're rather pressed for time –

JENNINGS: I take back what I said earlier about the Health Service – I take it back whole-heartedly… (*Tickled at his own joke.*) Whole-heartedly!

GIBBONS: I'm not sure you realise just how precarious your present situation is.

JENNINGS: Oh, I realise well enough! For the first time in my life I know what it feels like to be on the brink of something!

GIBBONS: Actually, that's what I wanted to talk to you about –

JENNINGS: (*Deaf.*) Do you have a charity of preference, Doctor?

GIBBONS: (*Cutting in.*) Would you please listen to me for a –

JENNINGS: (*Interrupting the interruption.*) I know it's hard for a man of the professions to accept handouts. Let's just say the next time you find yourself in legal hot water, not that you would – not a man of your stamp –

GIBBONS: There's something rather pressing I think you should know.

Something is wrong.

JENNINGS: (*Shrewdly.*) You put a black man's heart in? (*Undismayed.*) Splendid! Life's too short for unwarranted prejudice.

GIBBONS: No. It's nothing like that.

JENNINGS: (*A trifle deflated.*) Oh.

GIBBONS: You see, when we opened you up we found there was nothing there.

JENNINGS: No matter, no matter. The most important thing is that it's done, that's what it boils down to – the result – (*Dawning.*) I'm sorry…what did you say?

GIBBONS: First of all, let me make it clear that I've never been one to shirk responsibility. But some things are simply unavoidable. You see, from the X-ray we saw clearly that what we assumed to be the heart was situated on the left side of the thorax, but in actual fact…what we were seeing on the X-ray turned out to be not on the left at all.

JENNINGS: (*Confused.*) The heart?

GIBBONS: …Yes.

JENNINGS: Not on the left?

GIBBONS: No.

JENNINGS: It was on the wrong side?

GIBBONS: We call it dextrocardia. It's a congenital condition. Extremely rare.

JENNINGS: You didn't know this *before* you opened me up?

GIBBONS: As I say, it's extremely rare –

JENNINGS: You did do an X-ray?

GIBBONS: Of course.

JENNINGS: Wouldn't that make it fairly clear? I thought that was what an X-ray was for.

GIBBONS: I don't want to bore you with technicalities. Suffice to say it was nobody's fault. A straightforward example of Photo-Phobic-Inverted-Orienteering-Perception-Disorder on the part of the radiologist.

Pause.

JENNINGS: You looked at the X-ray the wrong way round.

GIBBONS: Not personally.

JENNINGS: (*Generously.*) Well, there's no use crying over split ribs. You got there in the end. Now the operation's done I wouldn't care if you told me I'd had a stone in there!

GIBBONS: Mr Jennings, I have some bad news for you.

Pause.

JENNINGS: (*Playful.*) It was a stone?

GIBBONS: No, it wasn't a stone.

JENNINGS: (*Suddenly serious, anticipating the worst.*) My wife's dead…

GIBBONS: (*Stopped in his tracks.*) She is?

JENNINGS: (*Confused.*) I don't know…

GIBBONS: (*Deeply alarmed.*) She's your wife, for Pete's sake!

JENNINGS: I thought that's what you were going to tell me –

GIBBONS: That she's your wife?

JENNINGS: That she's died in some horrible car crash –

GIBBONS: (*Genuinely shaken.*) Oh my God…

JENNINGS: I don't know if she has –

GIBBONS: But you think she might?

JENNINGS: I don't know!

GIBBONS: When did you hear?

JENNINGS: Just now –

GIBBONS: Who told you?

JENNINGS: You did!

GIBBONS: That she's dead?

JENNINGS: (*His worst fears confirmed.*) DEAD!

GIBBONS: I never said that!

JENNINGS: That's not what you were going to tell me?

GIBBONS: No!

JENNINGS: Thank God!

GIBBONS: So she's alright?

JENNINGS: I think so –

GIBBONS: What a relief! (*With genuine feeling.*) That could have been very tragic indeed.

Pause.

JENNINGS: You're sweating, Doctor. Are you sure you're well?

GIBBONS: (*Ploughing on.*) I'm fine… (*Looking at his watch.*) Look, Mr Jennings, I came to tell you something quite specific and we're running out of time –

JENNINGS: Relax, Doctor. Don't run yourself into the ground. Thanks to you the years stretch out before me!

GIBBONS: Mr Jennings, I want you to realise that this is as hard for me as it is for you, but…during the course of the operation, after we opened up the right side of the thorax after an initial blunder which – as I say – was not entirely our own –

JENNINGS: (*Chivvying.*) Yes, yes…

GIBBONS: Of course…well…it happened that once we exposed your right side, which is where the X-rays had initially indicated your heart would be… (*Pause.*) …I don't know quite how to put this…but we…well…

JENNINGS: Yes?

GIBBONS: Didn't find a heart at all.

JENNINGS tries to rationalise this news.

JENNINGS: You definitely looked?

GIBBONS: Oh yes.

JENNINGS: (*Helpfully.*) It wasn't tucked away somewhere? Behind a lung, perhaps?

GIBBONS looks seriously at him.

You must have found something. I was alive, wasn't I?

GIBBONS: In a manner of speaking.

JENNINGS: Well? There must have been something!

GIBBONS: Yes.

JENNINGS: Spit it out! Whatever it is, it can't be that bad…

GIBBONS: (*Directly.*) We found a bomb.

JENNINGS: …I'm still here!

Pause.

(*Hardly audible.*) A what?

GIBBONS: I'm so sorry.

Pause.

JENNINGS: Could you repeat that?

GIBBONS: Of course. (*Repeating exactly.*) We found a bomb.

JENNINGS: A…bomb?

GIBBONS: Yes.

JENNINGS: As in… (*Gestures an explosion.*)

GIBBONS nods solemnly.

A beat.

JENNINGS bursts out laughing.

Oh priceless! Oh, I like that! Very funny indeed…you chaps are a hoot!

JENNINGS laughs uproariously.

GIBBONS is not smiling.

Well go on, Doctor! Don't be such an old toad! I think it's brilliant! (*Imitating.*) 'You have a bomb instead of a heart, Mr Jennings.' I bet you tell all your patients that!

He laughs again.

GIBBONS: I wish I had better news.

JENNINGS' laughter gutters out.

I really don't know what else to say.

JENNINGS: You're serious.

GIBBONS: I'm afraid I am.

Pause.

JENNINGS: (*Tapping his chest in disbelief.*) In here?

GIBBONS: I wouldn't have believed it myself –

JENNINGS: You're pulling my leg!

GIBBONS: That's what the disposal squad told me.

JENNINGS: *Disposal squad!*

GIBBONS: Years of training, practice, experience. Nothing can prepare you for a thing like that. There we are in theatre: you laid out on the trolley. I'm ready – poised to sew the new heart in. Simple enough. Done it a thousand times. We know the drill. The team stands by. A man's life rests in our hands. Suddenly…alarm bells. Fire in the next-door theatre. I don't like to admit it. I'd like to think us masters of any situation. Yes, the bold ones tried to battle the fire. Others simply ran. As the Senior Consultant, the important thing was to keep calm, focused, never to lose sight of my…duty. It chokes me to say it, but I was deserted in your hour of need. It wasn't orderly. Pretty much a stampede, in fact. And yet in the eye of the storm, as the flames licked around us…there we were. You and I. (*Pause.*) Some moments in life are just that. Call it heroism if you will. But I weighed the options and found only one open to me. If I could stitch the new heart in – unaided – *solo*…by my reckoning I could still get you out of there safely before the fire spread. I prized open the ribs; peeled back the tissue. And there it was: a kilo of ticking Semtex.

Pause.

JENNINGS: 'Ticking'?

GIBBONS: It was all I could do to evacuate the hospital.

JENNINGS: 'Evacuate'?

GIBBONS: Total panic.

JENNINGS is struggling to visualise the scene.

JENNINGS: And you're quite sure it was a heart-shaped bomb? Not a bomb-shaped heart, for example?

GIBBONS: I've been a consultant for twelve years, Mr Jennings.

JENNINGS: I can imagine it can be quite confusing –

GIBBONS: I know a ventricular septum from a bicuspid valve.

JENNINGS: My mother has a rather large heart –

GIBBONS: I know a detonator when I see one.

JENNINGS: Detonator?

GIBBONS: Not something I wish to see again.

JENNINGS: What kind of a detonator?

GIBBONS: I'm not very up on explosives, myself. I know the bomb disposal boys cordoned off the area. After that it's a bit of a blur.

JENNINGS: It was *ticking*?

GIBBONS: It's rather outside my area of expertise, but I understand the device was definitely on a timer.

JENNINGS: You mean I could have been blown to bits? At any moment?

GIBBONS: That was my understanding.

JENNINGS: (*None of this making sense.*) But…how long had it been in there?

GIBBONS: Hard to tell.

JENNINGS: And they defused it?

GIBBONS: I'm not wholly familiar with the details, but from what I gather the device wasn't one they were familiar with. You must understand, Mr Jennings, this was a first for all of us.

JENNINGS: They left it…ticking? For you to take out?

GIBBONS: That was exactly the situation I was faced with, yes.

JENNINGS: Good heavens! I've never heard anything like it! You'll get an MBE! They would have left me in the lurch! So much for the security services! You know, it's fellows like you, Doctor – the professional underbelly of our society – without you this sickly herd would sniff its way to the gutter!

GIBBONS is troubled by the time.

You won't mind me asking how you got the bugger out? I should think there's been an awful hoo-ha in the press. I suppose there was a controlled explosion. Must have been a hell of a bang. I bet that attracted some publicity?

GIBBONS: It's been kept pretty hush-hush.

JENNINGS: My wife will be terribly worried –

GIBBONS: We thought it best not to inform her at the time.

JENNINGS: Probably wise.

GIBBONS: She is on her way now.

JENNINGS: Sylvie?

GIBBONS: She'll be arriving any minute.

Sound of a distant cry, off.

JENNINGS: What was that?

GIBBONS: Hm?

JENNINGS: That noise. It sounded like someone screaming.

GIBBONS: Hospital orderlies. They get raucous on payday.

JENNINGS looks up at the ceiling. He's suspicious. There's a camera in the corner of the room.

JENNINGS: The other room had windows.

GIBBONS: You're very safe here.

JENNINGS: (*Becoming anxious.*) The walls…they look thicker than before…the light – it's different.

GIBBONS: This is a secure ward.

JENNINGS takes in his surroundings for the first time.

JENNINGS: This isn't a hospital at all, is it? I don't even know you're a doctor. Where have you taken me? Where are we? (*The fog clears.*) Oh, I get it! You must think I'm quite a chump. You hear about these kinds of things on television. Pick on some chap when he's down – that'll bump up the ratings. It's 'NHS Big Brother'! That'll make Pick of the Day, I shouldn't wonder. Where are the cameras? Where are they? Come on! Funny-ha-ha. (*To the cameras.*) Funny-ha-ha-ha!

Another cry, off. Nearer this time.

You are to be congratulated on a genuine multi-media experience!

GIBBONS: Mr Jennings –

JENNINGS: (*Testily.*) You know, Doctor – if indeed you are a doctor – I've got better things to do with my time than listen to your claptrap. I'm grateful for the operation – don't get me wrong – but I never volunteered to participate in any television programme. I've got a wife and children to go home to!

JENNINGS rips away the sheets, intending to get up and leave.

GIBBONS: You can't.

He's right. JENNINGS is strapped to the bed. Thick leather bindings shackle his legs.

JENNINGS: What on earth…?!

GIBBONS: Will you listen to me for a moment –

JENNINGS: I can't move!

GIBBONS: Mr Jennings –

JENNINGS: (*Struggling.*) I'm strapped in!

GIBBONS: Charles, please –

JENNINGS: Don't 'Charles' me! Let me out, damn you!

GIBBONS: You must listen to me for a moment –

JENNINGS: I'm a lawyer! I know my rights! You can't imprison me in a television studio against my will! I never signed a release form! I'll make ribbons of you in court!

GIBBONS: You can't move –

JENNINGS: HELP! SOMEBODY!

GIBBONS: Nobody can hear you!

JENNINGS: (*Fortissimo.*) LET ME OUT!

GIBBONS: (*Matching him, with finality.*) THERE'S NOTHING YOU CAN DO TO STOP IT!

VOICE ON INTERCOM: DOCTOR GIBBONS TO THE COMMAND CENTRE IMMEDIATELY PLEASE.

Somewhere in the walls, speakers are hidden.

JENNINGS and GIBBONS stare at each other is silence, trembling slightly.

JENNINGS: (*With disbelief.*) Who was that?

GIBBONS: (*Urgent.*) Look, Charles, I did what any man would have done under the circumstances. Perhaps in time you'll understand that. There was no need for me to come here. But I wanted to break the news to you gently – to tell you you can go out with dignity. For Sylvie's sake if nothing else.

VOICE ON THE INTERCOM: (*Stern.*) DOCTOR GIBBONS TO THE COMMAND CENTRE.

JENNINGS is finding all this hard to swallow.

GIBBONS: Please don't make this harder for her than it already is.

JENNINGS: You did remove it? You cut it out?

GIBBONS: I was all in favour of it.

JENNINGS feels the left hand side of his chest.

(*Never one to miss a technicality.*) The other side.

JENNINGS: On a timer?

GIBBONS: As I say, the details of the explosive itself aren't really my field.

JENNINGS: YOU... (*He searches for sufficient opprobrium.*)...

GIBBONS: Please, Charles –

JENNINGS: YOU PERFECT –

GIBBONS: Keep calm –

JENNINGS: 'CALM'! I'M STRAPPED TO A BED IN A BUNKER WITH A BOMB NESTLING IN MY RIBS, AND YOU TELL ME TO KEEP CALM!

GIBBONS: You must understand – it could have blown me sky high!

JENNINGS: 'YOU'! What about ME? I demand to speak to someone in authority! I'm not prepared to live the rest of my life never knowing if the next moment will be my last!

GIBBONS: (*A shrug.*) That's life.

JENNINGS: That's intolerable!

GIBBONS: In your case, of course, it's also not technically correct.

JENNINGS: It's on a timer, isn't it – the device? It could go off right now! If you were a doctor you wouldn't come near me!

GIBBONS: There is some good news.

JENNINGS: 'Good'? What could possibly be good about this?

GIBBONS: They know when the timer's set for.

VOICE ON INTERCOM: (*Sternly.*) THANK YOU, DOCTOR GIBBONS.

GIBBONS: After all, you reap what you sow, don't you?

Blackout.

JENNINGS: What happened?

GIBBONS: They switched the lights off.

JENNINGS: Who are 'they'?

Pause.

Doctor?

Silence.

Doctor…

Silence.

For goodness' sake! (*Weakly at first, then crescendo.*) Help!… HELP ME! SOMEBODY HELP ME!

But only the echo of his voice and a deathly hush.

VOICE: (*Sinister and close.*) Save your breath.

JENNINGS: Doctor Gibbons?

VOICE: Got a long journey ahead.

JENNINGS: Who is that?

VOICE: The long, dark tunnel –

JENNINGS: Get away from me…

VOICE: A thousand virgins.

JENNINGS: I'm warning you!

VOICE: That's more your style, eh?

JENNINGS: Who are you?

VOICE: (*With venom.*) Your worst nightmare.

> *A noise like steel being sharpened.*

> Sharpening the shears…prodding and probing –

JENNINGS: No…

VOICE: Laughing and grinning, opening you up like a parcel –

JENNINGS: HELP!

VOICE: Holding your bleeding, throbbing heart in my hand –

JENNINGS: Get away from me!

VOICE: LIGHTS!

> *The lights flick on.*

> *JENNINGS is blinded and confused. Strapped to the bed, cowering from the light, he is utterly helpless and pathetic.*

> *AGENT PSMITH stands behind the bed, his arms raised in Messianic posture. Even standing as rigidly erect as he is, he is undeniably short. His voice betrays Cockney roots and shades of psychosis.*

> *The sharpening noise is created by running his metal comb along the iron bedstead.*

> *Gradually, JENNINGS' eyes readjust to the light.*

AGENT PSMITH runs the comb meticulously through his hair.

JENNINGS: (*Pathetically.*) What do you want?

PSMITH conjures a notebook from his pocket.

You've no right to keep me like this! I know my rights. I'm a lawyer – a QC!

AGENT PSMITH: (*From memory.*) Lombard Chambers, Middle Temple, Number 9, Harcourt Buildings.

JENNINGS: I demand to be released! You've no right to keep me like this!

AGENT PSMITH: 'Right'? What is a 'right', Mr Jennings?

JENNINGS: You have no right to keep me chained up!

AGENT PSMITH: Is it our 'right' to live in a safe, peaceful society? A society where you don't expect to be blown apart by a pair of unattended Nikes? I'd call that a 'right'. Wouldn't you agree? A community where you can assemble in licensed premises without fear you might…spruce up the cigarette machine with yer'innards. A society where you don't fear to put money in a parking meter, or help a small child, because some nutter's got you zeroed in his cross-hairs. That's what I call a right. Wouldn't you agree?

JENNINGS: Who are you?

AGENT PSMITH: Agent Psmith. (*Pause for dramatic effect.*) With a 'P'.

JENNINGS: Look here, Mr Smith –

AGENT PSMITH: *Agent* Psmith.

JENNINGS: Agent Smith –

AGENT PSMITH: With a 'P'.

JENNINGS: (*Ignoring him, with righteous indignation.*) My name is Charles Jennings. I have two small children. At some time in the past – exactly how long ago I no longer recall – I was admitted to St Miriam's Hospital for a heart transplant.

Just a minute ago I was in conference with a doctor – since vanished – who informed me that in place of a heart, I am apparently packed with explosive. Moreover, he indicated that the time of detonation is not entirely unknown – if indeed there is a bomb at all – which I doubt. I am lashed to a bed in what appears to be a bunker. Of you I know nothing except your unlikely name. Under the circumstances, I am doing my best to be civil. Unstrap me without delay from this bed and I'm prepared to forget this sorry episode ever occurred. Dally one second longer (*Pronouncing the P.*) P-Smithy old man, and I'll see to it that you never pollute the registers of employment again. Do I make myself clear?

AGENT PSMITH: Bravo, Mr Jennings! Bravo!

JENNINGS: You have no right to restrain me!

AGENT PSMITH: Tell you what: we'll make a deal. You want something from me. I want something from you. This Arab you've been on about. (*Opening his notebook.*) What does he look like?

JENNINGS: This what?

AGENT PSMITH: You heard.

JENNINGS: Which Arab?

AGENT PSMITH: I want to be gentle with you, I really do.

JENNINGS: I've no idea what you're talking about!

AGENT PSMITH: I see no reason why we shouldn't get along.

JENNINGS: I refuse to hold any sort of conversation whilst I am restrained illegally!

AGENT PSMITH: I-what?

JENNINGS: *Illegally!*

AGENT PSMITH considers.

AGENT PSMITH: You're unhappy about the status of your detention?

JENNINGS: I am not unhappy. I am spitting.

AGENT PSMITH: Gotcha.

PSMITH kneels and reaches under the bed.

JENNINGS: (*Relieved.*) Thank you. I'm not an unreasonable man and I am prepared to be lenient. I am not so naive as to think that mistakes don't occur in all walks of life. However, I must advise you that I intend to file a claim. I shall endeavour to keep your name out of it, bearing in mind your reasonable attitude.

AGENT PSMITH emerges from beneath the bed.

AGENT PSMITH: (*He hasn't heard.*) You what?

He is clutching a pair of large jump leads.

JENNINGS: (*Noticing the wires.*) What are those?

AGENT PSMITH: These?

JENNINGS: (*With mounting concern.*) Yes –

AGENT PSMITH: (*Simply.*) Cables.

He proceeds to attach them to JENNINGS' manacles.

JENNINGS: (*With increasing alarm.*) What…what are you doing?

AGENT PSMITH: Plugging it in.

JENNINGS: Plugging it in…plugging it in TO WHAT?!

PSMITH produces a power pack and tries to orientate the wires.

AGENT PSMITH: I never remember which way round they go…

JENNINGS: You can't seriously intend…stop that immediately! You can't possibly – this is preposterous – I'M WARNING YOU!

AGENT PSMITH: Please. I have delicate ears.

JENNINGS: You have no right! I thought you were going to release me!

AGENT PSMITH: Some people find it a release. Some people find it quite…pleasurable, in actual fact.

JENNINGS: (*The full implication dawning.*) You're not going…you don't seriously intend to…turn that thing on?

AGENT PSMITH: A little information. That's all I need.

JENNINGS: How dare you! That's torture!

AGENT PSMITH: No it's not. (*Beat.*) It's medication.

He hits the button sending a tester crackle of voltage through the wires.

JENNINGS: YAAOW!

JENNINGS convulses in agony.

The lights flicker.

AGENT PSMITH: (*Pleased it works.*) You are undergoing a programme of Electro-Convulsive Therapy. Established medical practice. If you answer my questions clearly then I will *not* administer the treatment. Failure to do so will initiate the healing process.

JENNINGS: You'll set it off!

AGENT PSMITH: Do what?

JENNINGS: If there is a bomb inside me you'll set it off, you fool! You'll kill us both!

AGENT PSMITH pauses.

AGENT PSMITH: Could have a point there.

He stands back, plugs his ears and administers another shock.

JENNINGS: YAAW!

AGENT PSMITH: (*Pleased.*) Nah. It's fine.

JENNINGS: …You will be held accountable! Mark my words! You are in breach of the Geneva Convention!

AGENT PSMITH: The what?

JENNINGS: The Geneva Convention!

AGENT PSMITH: Oh, grow up.

Another shock. Another scream.

JENNINGS: This is outrageous!

AGENT PSMITH: Let's get this straight: the first time you saw this Arab, what was he doing?

JENNINGS: (*Nursing his legs.*) It was a dream!

AGENT PSMITH: Perfectly admissible evidence.

JENNINGS: Since when?

AGENT PSMITH: Last week. Home Secretary's directive.

JENNINGS: For goodness' sake – it was probably something I saw on television – it's nothing significant!

AGENT PSMITH: Which channel?

JENNINGS: Does it matter?

AGENT PSMITH: (*With disdain.*) The BBC?

JENNINGS: Possibly.

Another shock.

Yes, the BBC!

AGENT PSMITH: (*Noting.*) No surprises there. And what did he look like?

JENNINGS: Who?

AGENT PSMITH: This Arab.

JENNINGS: You want me to describe a dream?

AGENT PSMITH: We can do a photo-fit if you'd prefer. Or we could turn up the voltage…

He goes for the power pack.

JENNINGS begins chattering to avoid further punishment.

JENNINGS: He was...big...like people are in dreams...

AGENT PSMITH: How big?

JENNINGS: I can't remember!

AGENT PSMITH: Bigger than the doctor?

JENNINGS: Bigger than you, certainly.

AGENT PSMITH: (*Impressed.*) That big?

JENNINGS: He wasn't a giant, I was just using you as a frame of reference –

AGENT PSMITH: You were lying down, were you not? When you saw him?

JENNINGS: I was asleep!

AGENT PSMITH: Exactly – so he might have looked bigger than he is, in reality.

JENNINGS: (*With deep frustration.*) It was a dream, for goodness sake!

AGENT PSMITH: What you're saying is, he might have been smaller than me?

JENNINGS: No!

AGENT PSMITH: I think you are.

JENNINGS: Fine! If it makes you feel better, he was Tom Thumb. Now will you please release these straps!

AGENT PSMITH: (*Interested.*) Tom-who?

JENNINGS: 'Thumb'! Thumb! The little chap. From the book –

AGENT PSMITH: The Koran?

JENNINGS: (*Exasperated.*) I can't remember who wrote it!

AGENT PSMITH: (*Conjuring a small microphone from a pocket.*) Check the Koran for references to 'thumb'. Some sort of code.

JENNINGS: (*Sanely.*) You're insane. I'm in a madhouse.

AGENT PSMITH: Get a grip, Mr Jennings. (*With venom.*) Or is it Jezeera?

JENNINGS can't believe what he's hearing. The pace of questioning increases.

When did they first approach you?

JENNINGS: Who?

AGENT PSMITH: Don't play games with me.

JENNINGS: The doctors?

AGENT PSMITH: (*Laced with mistrust.*) Them.

JENNINGS: If you're some sort of policeman I demand to see a warrant.

AGENT PSMITH: I don't need a warrant. You're in a hospital.

JENNINGS: Then if I'm not under arrest I demand to be released!

AGENT PSMITH: Of course you're under arrest.

JENNINGS: I haven't been read my rights!

AGENT PSMITH: Twice.

JENNINGS: When?

AGENT PSMITH: You were asleep.

JENNINGS: You can't arrest me in my sleep!

AGENT PSMITH: If you weren't going to explode I could hold you indefinitely.

JENNINGS: On what charge?

AGENT PSMITH: Deep suspicion.

JENNINGS: OF WHAT?

AGENT PSMITH: You may not look like one of them, but it's not what's on the outside any more, is it? It's what's ticking on the inside. The enemy's a slippery eel – changes his tactics daily. I have to admit, I did not anticipate the advance in weaponry that you represent. But if we have to open up every citizen of this country – open 'em right up and sift through 'em with…tweezers – if that's what it takes to beat the threat to our civilised society – if that's what it takes… then we will not flinch from our task. There's only a certain number of places you can hide a bomb. And we will win this war.

JENNINGS is beginning to grasp the situation.

JENNINGS: (*Relieved at the ridiculousness of it.*) You think I'm a terrorist.

AGENT PSMITH: Don't tell me: (*With disdain.*) 'Freedom Fighter'.

JENNINGS' laughter is sheer relief.

You find that humorous?

JENNINGS: I'm sorry! I don't mean to laugh. It's simply that there's been the most awful mix up. You can unplug the wires, now. If I knew what you were driving at in the first place I could have saved you the bother. Untie this lot and we'll all go home. Personally, I could do with a bath and a good square meal. I appreciate you people have to be vigilant. These are trying times. However, in this case you've simply got the wrong man.

Pause.

AGENT PSMITH: The wrong man?

JENNINGS: Yes.

AGENT PSMITH: Duff info?

JENNINGS: Precisely.

PSMITH considers the ramifications.

AGENT PSMITH: (*Reasonably.*) Alright. Prove it.

JENNINGS: Prove what?

AGENT PSMITH: You're not terroristic.

JENNINGS: (*On home ground.*) I'm afraid the burden of proof lies with you, old sport. If you accuse me of a crime, it's your obligation to prove those allegations beyond any reasonable doubt. That's how things work in this country, thank God.

AGENT PSMITH: Not anymore.

JENNINGS: Look it up.

AGENT PSMITH: Just did. The law has an obligation to adapt to the present situation. This is the era of pre-emptive action. No use putting bits of you on trial.

JENNINGS: I don't follow.

AGENT PSMITH: Now we've arrested you, it's up to *you* to prove to *us* you're not a terrorist.

JENNINGS: How can I? I'm strapped to this bed!

AGENT PSMITH: Exactly. Proves what a threat you are.

JENNINGS: I demand to see a lawyer!

AGENT PSMITH: You are a lawyer.

JENNINGS: Oh, this is absurd! I'm not a terrorist! Look at me! Do I look like a terrorist to you?

PSMITH sizes him up.

AGENT PSMITH: A potential terrorist, yes.

JENNINGS: Potential? You can arrest someone on the basis of what they *might* do? You'd have to arrest everybody!

AGENT PSMITH: (*Proudly.*) A thousand more agents are being recruited as we speak.

JENNINGS: This country has enjoyed unparalleled domestic peace!

AGENT PSMITH: And why? Because of the fine work being done by the men and women of our security forces. Thanks to their covert heroism the average Briton enjoys unrivalled stability.

JENNINGS: Does the concept of Civil Liberty mean nothing to you?

AGENT PSMITH: Britain is at war, Mr Jennings.

JENNINGS: With who?

AGENT PSMITH: That's classified information.

JENNINGS: 'Classified'? How can it be classified?

AGENT PSMITH: For the first time in the history of this nation we're fighting a war on *no fronts*, as a direct result of which… our resources are stretched to the limit. If the rank and file knew who the enemy was, he might find out we were after him. And where's the element of surprise in that?

JENNINGS: Look, Mr Psmith –

AGENT PSMITH: *Agent* Psmith.

JENNINGS: Agent Psmith, I'm a decent, law-abiding member of the general public and a practising barrister. I came in for a vital heart transplant –

AGENT PSMITH: (*Smugly.*) Tactical error.

JENNINGS: I saw nothing unusual in the run up to the operation –

AGENT PSMITH: Nothing at all?

JENNINGS: No!

AGENT PSMITH: Didn't strike you the nurse was a bit…friendly?

JENNINGS: Nurse Davids?

AGENT PSMITH: You walked into a honey trap, Jezeera!

JENNINGS: (*Reeling.*) A what?

AGENT PSMITH: We've been tailing you for months.

JENNINGS: Nurse Davids?

AGENT PSMITH: Admirably dedicated to her job. Took you in hook, line and sinker – if you'll pardon the expression.

JENNINGS: Nurse Davids! A honey trap? But she's amnesiac – I prosecuted her!

AGENT PSMITH: That's right: morally lapsed with a brain like an Etch-a-Sketch. A model operative. We've had intelligence for months that extremist elements have been planning an attack on a soft target. All we needed was the tip-off.

JENNINGS: Tip-off?

AGENT PSMITH: After that it was plain sailing.

JENNINGS: *Tip-off from who?*

AGENT PSMITH: (*Tempted.*) ...What kind of a monkey do you take me for?

JENNINGS: I came in for an operation!

AGENT PSMITH: And that's what you call gratitude, is it? That's how you thank our public services? I've never understood the mindset, myself. You see it on TV – reports of the families weeping and wailing – euphoric 'cos their little Mohammed's popped himself in a busy shopping centre, or some distant cousin's sponging bits of his sister off the floor, weeping for the sheer privilege of it –

JENNINGS: What's that got to do with *me*?

AGENT PSMITH: (*Losing himself for a moment.*) Shut it, Jesus!

JENNINGS: My name's Jennings!

AGENT PSMITH: Look...chum – this may be a religious war for you. But you show me one Church of England Bishop, strapping up the head chorister like a tiny Guy Fawkes –

JENNINGS: You've got it all wrong! You don't understand!

AGENT PSMITH: That's it, isn't it? That's the argument! 'You don't understand!' We Westerners don't understand the way your Muslimistic minds work; the way you crucify your kosher meat 'til it practically waltzes out the mosque; the way you circumcise your Lamas with that funny little knife you ram down your lederhosen. Well, that's exactly where you're wrong! We do understand. I'm not a religious man – I go to Matins every so often – but it's fairly clear to me and I've read it in a number of books: *there is only one God.* Not the thirty-six million little Buddhas that you and your Moonie fundamentalistics marry yourselves off for!

Another cry, off.

PSMITH has worked himself into a lather.

(*Collecting himself.*) I can turn that bomb off, you know. A little information, that's all I need.

JENNINGS: Defuse it?

AGENT PSMITH: Flick of a switch.

JENNINGS: The doctor said they couldn't –

AGENT PSMITH: Doctor Gibbons means well, bless him, but he's not…senior, if you know what I mean. Out the loop. Paid by the hour. Privileged access and all.

JENNINGS: (*Getting it straight.*) If I give you the information you need, you can defuse the bomb?

AGENT PSMITH: Now you're gettin' it.

JENNINGS: You'll let me go? I can go back to my life as if none of this ever happened?

AGENT PSMITH: Easy as pie.

JENNINGS: (*Indicating the power supply.*) You promise you won't… do that again?

AGENT PSMITH: Not unless you ask for it.

AGENT PSMITH looks at his watch.

JENNINGS: How do I know you're not lying?

AGENT PSMITH administers a shock.

YAAW! YOU GAVE ME YOUR WORD!

AGENT PSMITH: (*Logically.*) You asked for that.

JENNINGS: All RIGHT! Go ahead – whatever you need to ask. I'll do my best.

AGENT PSMITH flicks to the relevant page of his notebook.

AGENT PSMITH: Do you know any Islamicistic people?

JENNINGS: Any what?

AGENT PSMITH: (*Clarifying.*) Anyone you know holiday in Mecca?

JENNINGS is stunned by the question.

(*Tapping his watch.*) Time is ticking, Jezebel.

AGENT PSMITH goes for the button.

JENNINGS: NO! Hold on – wait – there was a fellow, someone I represented…he owned a shop. His daughter went to university with the son of a friend of mine. I think he was a Muslim.

AGENT PSMITH: D'he wear a skull-cap?

JENNINGS: (*Perplexed by the question.*) No.

AGENT PSMITH: Turban?

JENNINGS: He wasn't a Sikh –

AGENT PSMITH: Didn't wear a hat?

JENNINGS: Not that I can remember.

AGENT PSMITH: He's definitely fundamentalistic?

JENNINGS: He seemed perfectly normal to me.

AGENT PSMITH takes notes.

AGENT PSMITH: What kind of a shop d'he run?

JENNINGS: It wasn't really a shop. More of a travel agent.

AGENT PSMITH: (*Knowingly.*) Ah.

JENNINGS: Tiny place, bucket shop.

AGENT PSMITH: Sell flights?

JENNINGS: I suppose he must have.

AGENT PSMITH: Hold a pilot's licence, did he?

JENNINGS: I doubt it.

AGENT PSMITH: Driving licence?

JENNINGS: Yes –

AGENT PSMITH: Where did he learn to drive?

JENNINGS: I have no idea.

AGENT PSMITH: (*Forcefully.*) Guess.

JENNINGS: I really don't –

> *Another shock.*

> (*The first thing that comes to mind.*) BSM!

AGENT PSMITH: A group of them? Learning together were they? At the school?

JENNINGS: How should I know?

AGENT PSMITH: (*Piecing together the clues.*) B-S-M… Bin… Something… Mm…

JENNINGS: I really don't see that this is going to be any use to you –

AGENT PSMITH: The charge?

JENNINGS: What?

AGENT PSMITH: You said he was in court.

JENNINGS: Yes. Fraud.

AGENT PSMITH: Got him off, did you?

JENNINGS: He should never have been charged in the first place.

AGENT PSMITH: (*Under his breath.*) Put that right.

JENNINGS: What did you just say?

AGENT PSMITH: (*Ploughing on.*) Big fella, was he?

JENNINGS: Medium build. Bigger than you.

AGENT PSMITH: (*Sensitive to such comments.*) Yes, yes, alright…and his name, this A-rab?

JENNINGS: He wasn't an Arab!

Another shock.

ALRIGHT! HE WAS AN ARAB!

AGENT PSMITH: Name?

JENNINGS: I don't remember. It was a long time ago! Now please, NO MORE!

Pause.

AGENT PSMITH: Do you know what's going to happen at two o'clock?

JENNINGS: Lunch?

AGENT PSMITH: I have lunch, yes.

JENNINGS: What about me?

Beat.

AGENT PSMITH: (*In the style of so many movies.*) You're gonna blow.

JENNINGS: WHAT?

AGENT PSMITH: I'd start talking if I was you.

JENNINGS: TWO O'CLOCK?! But that's in… (*He grabs the alarm clock from the bedside table.*) …that's in forty-three minutes!

AGENT PSMITH: (*Checking his wristwatch.*) Forty-four. That clock's fast.

JENNINGS: You've got to stop it!

AGENT PSMITH: Just as soon as you give me the information I need.

JENNINGS: (*In despair.*) JESUS!

AGENT PSMITH: (*Noting.*) And his surname?

JENNINGS: What?

AGENT PSMITH: The Arab.

JENNINGS: I don't know!

AGENT PSMITH: (*Wearily.*) I don't want to pick bits of you off this ceiling, Jethro. Not after lunch.

PSMITH goes for the button…

JENNINGS: ALRIGHT! (*Calmer.*) His name was Allan.

AGENT PSMITH: (*Noting.*) Jesus…Allan.

JENNINGS: Allan Jones. Something like that.

AGENT PSMITH: Jones?

JENNINGS: Yes, Jones. His name was Allan Jones – now will you please switch this thing off!

Pause.

AGENT PSMITH: Where'd he come from?

JENNINGS: (*Plucking it out of the air.*) Cardiff…

AGENT PSMITH: An immigrant?

JENNINGS: (*Facetiously.*) Yes! He rafted across the Severn.

AGENT PSMITH: Makes sense. And you think he might have connections with other mentalists?

JENNINGS: Almost certainly! Now will you please get someone to defuse this infernal thing!

AGENT PSMITH: All in good time –

JENNINGS: There isn't any time! There's only…forty-two minutes to go –

AGENT PSMITH: (*Correcting him.*) Forty-three.

JENNINGS: (*Desperate.*) I've given you the man's name – he is a terrorist! He admitted as much to me at the time! He had a picture of the Pentagon in flames as his screen saver. In his lunch break he destroyed major American landmarks in imaging software programmes. What more do you want?

AGENT PSMITH: (*To himself.*) Good with computers. (*To JENNINGS.*) I suppose he's the one who installed your device?

JENNINGS: I don't know! I'm as confused as you are!

AGENT PSMITH: (*Firmly.*) I'm not at all confused.

JENNINGS: What do you want me to say?

AGENT PSMITH: Say, 'He installed it.'

JENNINGS: He did! He installed it! I remember!

AGENT PSMITH: (*Putting words into his mouth.*) He's the Arab… from the dream?

JENNINGS: YES! Now will you please –

AGENT PSMITH: And his name's Allan?

JENNINGS: Well done!

AGENT PSMITH: Which is clearly the anglicised version of his Hasidic name… (*He's piecing this together.*) …Allan…Allah… Al Jones! A sheikh! He co-ordinates a cell! He's got a network of agents across the country –

JENNINGS: Hold on a minute –

AGENT PSMITH: He's planning a gas attack on the underground –

JENNINGS: No!

AGENT PSMITH: In a fairground!

JENNINGS: No!

AGENT PSMITH: Chelsea football ground!

JENNINGS: Look –

AGENT PSMITH: (*Triumphant.*) I knew it! (*Into his microphone.*) Cancel all sporting events until further notice. Close all roads and airports. Imminent threat: Bikini Red.

AGENT PSMITH makes hasty notes.

JENNINGS watches him, thunderstruck.

JENNINGS: To watch you work is to wonder if the term 'Intelligence Service' is not a colossal misnomer.

Another shock.

WILL YOU PLEASE STOP DOING THAT!

AGENT PSMITH: (*Holding his ears.*) Does your wife know about your political activities?

JENNINGS: She doesn't know anything! (*With real concern.*) She's going to be terribly worried…

AGENT PSMITH: Not easy for her, mind. Lining the nest for a pair of fledgling Imams…couple of tiny Mullahs. Gotta be tough.

JENNINGS: (*With real anger.*) I swear – you lay one finger on my children –

AGENT PSMITH: Like the cinema do you, Mr Jennings?

JENNINGS: What?

PSMITH reveals a screen which has until now remained hidden in the wall.

AGENT PSMITH: (*Pronouncing it clearly.*) Cin-e-ma. The flicks. Munch munch. Wine gums. Sticky seats. The 'movies'?

JENNINGS: What on earth – ?

AGENT PSMITH: I like a good movie, me.

JENNINGS: This thing goes off in thirty-nine
minutes –

AGENT PSMITH: That one with…um…oh…who is it…?

JENNINGS: If you don't switch it off now, it'll be too late!

AGENT PSMITH: (*Needing help.*) Come on…

JENNINGS: (*Spelling it out for him.*) MY LIFE IS IN YOUR HANDS!

AGENT PSMITH: Big teeth, hat, dances a lot…

JENNINGS: (*Reflex.*) Gene Kelly?

AGENT PSMITH: That's the one –

JENNINGS: You're insane!

AGENT PSMITH: Lights!

The lights dim.

JENNINGS: For goodness' sake!

AGENT PSMITH: Make yourself comfortable. (*Of the buttons on the remote control.*) I never remember which one… Why don't they just write 'Play'?

JENNINGS: Honestly, there's isn't time –

A picture appears on the screen.

AGENT PSMITH: (*Showing him the button.*) That one.

The film now playing on the screen appears to be some sort of home video.

The camera swings amateurishly round an amusement park, settling on a woman and two small boys. The camera zooms in jerkily.

JENNINGS: (*To the screen.*) Sylvie! (*To PSMITH.*) Where did you get this…?

AGENT PSMITH: It's not on general release.

JENNINGS: How dare you! This is a private video!

The boys have noticed that they are being filmed and turn to wave into the camera. They are calling 'Daddy!'

Harry...Sam...

AGENT PSMITH: (*Fiddling with the remote.*) Could be a bit brighter.

JENNINGS: This is private property!

Harry waves at the camera.

AGENT PSMITH: (*Of Harry.*) Got your mouth, look.

Now Sam waves. He seems to be waving directly at JENNINGS.

The camera tilts up to frame Sylvie, who waves too.

JENNINGS: This is perfectly monstrous!

AGENT PSMITH: Family trip, was it?

JENNINGS: What do you want me to say?

AGENT PSMITH: If it was a family trip, say it was a family trip.

JENNINGS: It's Alton Towers, for Christ's sake!

The camera has dropped to film the pavement.

It was my son's birthday! We went on a family outing –

AGENT PSMITH: His idea of a good time, is it? A recce?

JENNINGS: He's four years old!

AGENT PSMITH: (*Calculating.*) Scorpio...

JENNINGS: Families across the world take videos like this every day!

AGENT PSMITH: Exactly.

JENNINGS: What do you mean 'exactly'? It's a home video!

AGENT PSMITH: That's what gives it away! You dress it up as a bog-standard family vid. Course you do. Common sense. You wouldn't write 'Training Video' all over it –

JENNINGS: It's not a training video!

AGENT PSMITH: Course it's not. It's such a dead ringer for a family vid, it's got 'casing job' written all over it.

JENNINGS: I can't win!

Another shock.

AGENT PSMITH: It's not a game, Muktar. There's lives at stake.

JENNINGS is starting to crack.

JENNINGS: My eyes…

AGENT PSMITH: Who's that?

PSMITH stills the film. In the background a man sells candyfloss from a stall.

JENNINGS: I can't focus…

AGENT PSMITH: (*Pointing at the man.*) There.

JENNINGS: Please!

AGENT PSMITH: Candyfloss man.

JENNINGS: I can't see…

AGENT PSMITH: (*Looking closely.*) Looks like a Jones to me. Mufti, of course.

JENNINGS: I'M IN PAIN! Do you comprehend that?

AGENT PSMITH: (*Mishearing.*) A rendezvous?

JENNINGS: I have no idea –

A shock.

It's just somebody who was there!

AGENT PSMITH: Change my mind about switching you off –

JENNINGS: ALRIGHT!

Pause.

(*Sadly.*) That's him. That's Jones.

AGENT PSMITH: 'There's a song in my heart and I'm ready for love.' Lights!

The lights snap up. PSMITH puts away the screen. JENNINGS can barely move.

You've been most helpful, Mr Jennings.

JENNINGS: (*Weakly.*) You'll let me go?

AGENT PSMITH: I'll do better than that. I shall be putting you forward for immunity.

JENNINGS: You will?

AGENT PSMITH: Posthumously, yes.

VOICE ON INTERCOM: AGENT PSMITH TO THE COMMAND CENTRE.

JENNINGS: (*Crushed.*) I've told you everything I know –

AGENT PSMITH: The truth is, you people have become too advanced for your own good. That piece you're packing is years ahead of its time. The only man who could defuse you is the man who installed you.

JENNINGS: There must be a way to stop it!

AGENT PSMITH: (*Looking at his watch.*) Any last requests?

JENNINGS: You can't leave me like this!

VOICE ON INTERCOM: THANK YOU, AGENT PSMITH. THAT WILL BE ALL.

JENNINGS: That's it? It's over? Just like that? There's nothing you can do?

AGENT PSMITH: Sorry chum.

PSMITH turns to go.

JENNINGS struggles to come to terms with the terror of his predicament.

JENNINGS: There is one thing – the doctor…he said my wife… Sylvie…he said she was on her way here. Is that true?

AGENT PSMITH: Knowing the doctor as I do… I'd say…unlikely.

JENNINGS: (*All pride gone.*) I WANT HER HERE! I want Sylvie! I want to see my wife!

AGENT PSMITH: I can take a message.

JENNINGS: IS IT TOO MUCH TO ASK?

A cry, off, accompanied by the sound of a sharp crackle.

This time the lights flicker and go out, plunging the room into darkness once more.

AGENT PSMITH: Night night, Jezeera.

PSMITH disappears.

All alone, JENNINGS cries out.

JENNINGS: Let me OUT! Let me GO! You have no right!… (*He sobs.*) …my boys…my beautiful boys… (*Hopelessly.*) SYLVIE! HELP ME! PLEASE…GOD! SOMEONE! …HELP ME!

His sobbing chokes the darkness.

End of Act One.

ACT TWO

A torch beam cuts the darkness. The beam jolts its way across the cell, revealing bright frames of a trembling, disorientated JENNINGS. A hand reaches up to open a small fuse box on the wall. A switch flicks. The lights snap up. The hand holding the torch belongs to a man with a rigid back and military bearing. He holds a torch in one hand and in the other a briefcase, which he lays down neatly. He is wearing fatigues.

LOVEDAY: Please accept my sincere apologies for the delay in getting here, Mr Jennings. The slightest surge in current and the trip switch goes down like a startled rabbit. I've said as much to Maintenance.

He can see JENNINGS' pitiful condition now.

Mr Jennings?

JENNINGS: (*Incoherent.*) ...can't take...any more...

COLONEL LOVEDAY observes JENNINGS carefully.

LOVEDAY: (*With concern.*) Mr Jennings, can you hear me?

JENNINGS: Do anything...

LOVEDAY: (*Slowly.*) Can you understand what I'm saying to you?

JENNINGS: (*Delirious.*) ...Jones...it's Jones...

LOVEDAY: Dear me.

LOVEDAY moves towards the power pack.

JENNINGS panics.

JENNINGS: NO! PLEASE! NOT ANY MORE! I CAN'T TAKE IT! I BEG YOU!

LOVEDAY: (*Kindly.*) It's quite alright.

LOVEDAY unplugs the leads from the pack and approaches JENNINGS' bed.

JENNINGS flinches in terror.

I'm here now. Everything is in hand.

He detaches the cables from the shackles and puts the whole device safely away.

There'll be no more of this, I assure you.

LOVEDAY retrieves a bottle of water from his briefcase. Hands it to JENNINGS.

JENNINGS is suspicious.

Go ahead. Please.

A moment. Then JENNINGS drinks thirstily. Revives a little.

JENNINGS: Who are you?

LOVEDAY: My name is Colonel Loveday. I am personally responsible for the smooth running of operations here at B.I.F. It is my duty to ensure that our residents are treated with the hospitality they deserve.

Another longer cry, off.

JENNINGS: What is this place?

LOVEDAY: You are a guest of Her Majesty's Battlefield Interrogation Facility, or 'B.I.F.' as we like to call her.

JENNINGS: (*Faltering with relief and nervous emotion.*) I've been tortured…

LOVEDAY: Mr Jennings, your treatment has been a disgrace.

JENNINGS: Plugged in, electrocuted – multiple times –

LOVEDAY: This is precisely why I'm here. To listen to your grievances and make a full report.

LOVEDAY retrieves an official casebook from his briefcase. He makes notes conscientiously.

JENNINGS: I've been chained to this bed –

LOVEDAY: (*Wincing in sympathy.*) Brutal – no other word.

JENNINGS: These straps are cutting into my ankles –

LOVEDAY: (*Sucking air.*) Htts…

JENNINGS: (*Encouraged.*) I've had nothing to eat since I arrived! I have been denied contact with my family! Disorientated! I've been intimidated, abused…words shoved into my mouth –

LOVEDAY: (*Noting, encouraging.*) As much detail as possible.

JENNINGS: I don't know where I am! Or if anyone in the outside world even knows I'm here at all! I've been repeatedly denied access to a lawyer! I have reason to believe my house has been searched and still I have no idea under what charges I am being held! Since the moment I awoke, I have been treated in a degrading and inhuman manner! I demand to be released!

LOVEDAY: Under the circumstances, may I say you are being eminently reasonable.

JENNINGS: I have been repeatedly told that I am being medically treated. I am not! I have been lied to at every step of the way! My treatment has been nothing short of barbaric!

LOVEDAY: Mr Jennings, as a representative of Her Majesty's Government, I am more ashamed than I can express that these outrages happened on my watch. I accept *full* responsibility. You can rest assured that I shall track down the perpetrators of this brutality and bring them to justice. To speak for myself… I am in moral shock. You are, in a sense, one of us. This kind of inhumanity represents a stain on all our consciences. Your case will prove the litmus test for this government's views on human rights. I shall be initiating an internal inquiry to find the culprit as soon as it's feasible to do so.

JENNINGS: There's no need for an inquiry –

LOVEDAY: I'm sorry?

JENNINGS: I said there's no need for an inquiry –

LOVEDAY: *Au contraire*! There is every need for an inquiry, Mr Jennings! I shall see to it personally that the Prime Minister is informed of your treatment immediately after the next election.

JENNINGS: I can tell you who did it to me! He called himself Psmith. He was here a minute ago –

LOVEDAY: (*Filing the notes away.*) As I say, the committee will publish its findings in full, in secret, in due course.

JENNINGS: You'll catch him – he'll be out there in the corridor! He disappeared when the lights went off. They were calling him –

LOVEDAY: Who was calling him?

JENNINGS: The voices –

LOVEDAY: (*With concern.*) 'Voices'?

JENNINGS: In the wall!

LOVEDAY: I see. What did you say his name was?

JENNINGS: Psmith. With a silent 'P'.

LOVEDAY: Strikes me as a faintly ridiculous name.

JENNINGS: (*Helpfully.*) It's a code name –

LOVEDAY: You didn't get his full details?

JENNINGS: He was electrocuting me!

LOVEDAY: Pity.

JENNINGS: You can't miss him: short man, deranged look – greasy hair…wearing a suit –

LOVEDAY: I'm afraid that doesn't really narrow it down.

Another cry, off. The lights flicker.

JENNINGS: That'll be him now! He's probably torturing some other poor bastard!

LOVEDAY: The truth is, Mr Jennings, you have been the unfortunate victim of what we call in the business a 'bad apple'. I'm not here to make excuses. Every breach of code shakes the foundations of common decency we're here to defend. I can assure you that your complaints have been duly noted. Though to put it objectively: one bad apple doesn't make a rotten strudel. Wouldn't you agree?

JENNINGS: I have been the victim of the most callous brutalisation! Not to mention a catalogue of offences in breach of the Human Rights Act, Articles Three and Four of the Geneva Convention –

LOVEDAY: If you'll allow me to stop you there, Mr Jennings – and after all, time is one of our many enemies – this is the post-nine-eleven world we're talking about. The gloves are off. Now, I'm not defending the actions of a loose apple – of course I'm not. It's the age-old conundrum: would you slit's a child's throat to save a nation? Or rather, to give a more pertinent example, if you know the whereabouts of another suicide bomber like yourself, for instance –

JENNINGS: I'm not a suicide bomber!

LOVEDAY: Hear me out, please. And this bomber was very shortly going to tear a crowd of Sunday shoppers to ribbons, let us say – are we morally right, or morally wrong, to ensure that we save the lives of those innocents, even if it means electrocuting you? I'm not in favour of torture – not by a long chalk. But you must appreciate that there are…grey areas. Sometimes, on the bad days, I feel like blowing myself up. It's perfectly natural. The difference between us is that I know, deep down, it's not on. Very much *off*, in fact.

JENNINGS: You appear to be a rational man, Colonel. I apologise if I sound hysterical, but I have been tortured by a moron. Throughout the entire time that I have been strapped into this bed, not a single shred of evidence has been produced against me. I still have no idea under what trumped up charge I am being held – if indeed there is a charge at all –

LOVEDAY: I do understand your frustration –

JENNINGS: YOU DO NOT UNDERSTAND! YOU DO NOT UNDERSTAND AT ALL!

LOVEDAY takes a paper from his briefcase.

LOVEDAY: Am I right in saying that you recently wrote a letter to *The Times* newspaper?

JENNINGS is baffled by the non-sequitur.

JENNINGS: What's that got to do with this?

LOVEDAY: Would you say that the contents of that letter are representative of your political views as a whole?

JENNINGS: I –

LOVEDAY: (*Reading.*) 'Dear Sir' – you write on the twelfth of March –

JENNINGS: (*Stupefied.*) Where did you find that?

LOVEDAY: 'The recent spate of repressive legislation, directed against an apparent' – italicised – 'threat to this country can only exacerbate the problem.' Wonderful word, 'exacerbate'. (*Continuing.*) 'Should this repression of our most basic liberties continue, we the ordinary men and women of this country will be forced to take matters into our own hands.' Given your situation, Mr Jennings, that's a fairly conclusive manifesto.

JENNINGS: You missed out the last sentence –

LOVEDAY: As a statement of intent, I can't imagine anything clearer.

JENNINGS: I said we'd be forced to *vote* for a party that would reinstate those liberties –

LOVEDAY: (*Nipping him in the bud.*) It is my duty to ensure that the public remains safe, Mr Jennings! That is my *raison d'être*. The reality is that the nature of the threat we're facing does not allow for shilly-shallying. There can be no half-measures. You are a prime example: at what point does a letter writer become a parcel bomber? When does libertarian become Nitroglycerine? When does protest become Semtex? At what point does the conviction you are right…become… Gelignite?

JENNINGS: I have the right to a legal trial!

LOVEDAY: Tell me one thing, if you will. Is there a more inalienable right in our society than the right to be safe? I don't think I'm alone in that opinion. It's easy to single out the abuses, the anomalies, the black sheep –

JENNINGS: I refuse to play any part in this trumped up, kangaroo court!

LOVEDAY: You may not believe me, Mr Jennings, but I was weaned on a diet of *laissez-faire* –

JENNINGS: Unless you intend to formally charge me –

LOVEDAY: I value anything-goes as much as the next man. If I sleep soundly, it's because I know that if we don't act firmly and promptly there will be no 'faire' to 'laissez'. There will be nothing left to 'go'.

JENNINGS: That doesn't change the fact –

LOVEDAY: You think I don't cringe at this?

He produces JENNINGS' 'Get Well' card from his briefcase. It's in a transparent bag.

In the foreground...a woman. Behind her, a building – large in scale...almost certainly a house. But potentially...you must recognise...a target. In this corner, the sun, drawn with radiating streaks of thick yellow reaching almost to the structure –

JENNINGS: You can't be serious?

LOVEDAY: A sun most likely – a perfectly innocent sun, I don't doubt, but possibly – just possibly...a nuclear device.

JENNINGS: It's a 'Get Well' card!

LOVEDAY: Most probably.

JENNINGS: It's drawn in crayon –

LOVEDAY: (*Meaningfully.*) By your son, Mr Jennings. Now put yourself in my shoes –

JENNINGS: (*Ugly.*) Aalright!

LOVEDAY: The inevitable inquiry –

JENNINGS: I hear you!

LOVEDAY: Heads will roll. For the sake of safety I cannot ignore –

JENNINGS: FINE! Let's play it your way. Firstly – (*Mockingly.*) Your Honour – if I may speak for the defence, lashed as I am to this medieval pallet – my son is six years old. Secondly – m' lord – he is not a criminal – potential or otherwise. I can provide witnesses to the effect that his range of operations has been hitherto confined to the crèche. As for his intentions in designing that card – (*Acid.*) Exhibit A – I humbly suggest that they derive from the basic human emotion we refer to in my household as *care*.

LOVEDAY: Tush now. Let's not make a spectacle of this –

JENNINGS: Care, you hear me?

LOVEDAY: Yes, I hear you –

JENNINGS: I'm coming in, am I?

LOVEDAY: Loud and clear.

JENNINGS: No need to pipe up for the galleries?

LOVEDAY: We're a little too old for playtime, Mr Jennings –

JENNINGS: YOU THINK THIS IS PLAYTIME? You think this is funny? I put it before this non-existent court that your nightmarish interpretation of unsubstantiated evidence would indeed be laughable, were it not for my savage predicament. 'Abuse of Process' doesn't come close. I defy you, Colonel, to show me one piece of evidence beyond this concocted nonsense to suggest that I am anything but –

LOVEDAY: Come now, Mr Jennings –

JENNINGS: – an innocent victim!

LOVEDAY: At the risk of sounding simplistic –

JENNINGS: I'VE DONE NOTHING WRONG!

Pause.

LOVEDAY: I see.

LOVEDAY produces a form from his briefcase. He adopts the manner of cross-examining counsel.

Is this the testimony you signed on entering the hospital?

He shows it to JENNINGS.

JENNINGS: It was a medical questionnaire –

LOVEDAY: When asked about your connections with banned organisations, you singled out the MCC.

JENNINGS: That was a joke!

LOVEDAY: For you, perhaps. (*Steaming on.*) In this same document, you deny any specialist weapons training, despite the fact that you are a bomb. What am I to make of that? Hm?

JENNINGS: I am not the enemy!

LOVEDAY: (*Producing another document.*) 'This is the wake-up call…the call to arms! This is the new beginning!' Isn't that what you said to Doctor Gibbons? Come on, Mr Jennings. You're an intelligent man. I don't need to spell it out, do I?

JENNINGS: (*To the heavens.*) Why me?

LOVEDAY: That, Mr Jennings, is the million dollar question. But as you know, time is ticking and there are a few odds and ends to straighten up before we let you go. One or two bits of paperwork. Then we're done.

LOVEDAY rummages in his briefcase.

JENNINGS: 'Done'?

LOVEDAY: (*Affirmative.*) Ah-huh.

JENNINGS: As in…finished?

LOVEDAY: Yes.

JENNINGS: You'll let me go?

LOVEDAY: I've no intention of hanging on to you.

JENNINGS: What about the bomb? Psmith said it would go off in forty-three minutes – he said two o'clock –

LOVEDAY: Ah, yes. Thank you for reminding me. It seems now, with the benefit of hindsight, that the forty-three-minute claim was probably inaccurate. On the information we had in front of us at the time, it seemed perfectly feasible that you might indeed explode in forty-three minutes. At the time, two o'clock seemed as good an estimate as any.

JENNINGS: You didn't know for sure?

LOVEDAY: We had pretty strong whiffs.

JENNINGS: 'Whiffs'? It's my life you're talking about!

LOVEDAY: Quite. Which is why I am pleased to announce that you will not be detonating at two o'clock this afternoon.

Beat.

JENNINGS: I won't?

LOVEDAY: No.

JENNINGS: (*The relief overwhelming.*) Thank God…

LOVEDAY: By the latest estimate, you're due to go off at five-to. As I say, I accept full responsibility for any inconvenience we may have caused.

JENNINGS picks up the alarm clock in disbelief.

JENNINGS: Five-to? THAT'S IN TWENTY-SIX MINUTES!

LOVEDAY: (*Checking his watch.*) Twenty-seven. But I take your point. We are pressed for time.

LOVEDAY produces a document from his briefcase and a fountain pen from his pocket.

I'd like you to sign this for me, if you would.

JENNINGS: You deceitful –

LOVEDAY: Now, now. There's no reason why this can't be handled in a perfectly civil fashion –

JENNINGS: (*Struggling.*) LET ME GO THIS INSTANT!

LOVEDAY: The quicker we get through this, the more time you'll have with your wife.

JENNINGS stops struggling.

JENNINGS: Sylvie?

LOVEDAY: She's right outside.

JENNINGS: (*A ray of hope.*) Sylvie!

LOVEDAY: The sooner we get this done, the sooner I can show her in.

LOVEDAY holds the paper for JENNINGS to sign.

JENNINGS tries to read it.

JENNINGS: I haven't got my glasses.

LOVEDAY: Red tape. Nothing more. Sign there and it's all wrapped up.

JENNINGS: (*Reading, squinting.*) 'I, Charles Harley Brooke Jennings, in the name of Allah the Great, the All-Powerful' – (*Breaking off.*) What is this?

LOVEDAY: Carry on. It picks up.

JENNINGS: (*Reading.*) 'I, Charles Harley Brooke Jennings, in the name of Allah the Great, the All-Powerful, hereby declare that I attempted to detonate myself inside a flagship hospital of the British National Health Service.' (*Breaking off.*) I'm not putting my name to this rubbish!

LOVEDAY: On second thoughts, 'explode' would be better than 'detonate'. Punchier.

JENNINGS thinks carefully. Then slowly, deliberately, he tears the paper into tiny pieces, defiantly holding LOVEDAY's gaze as he does so. He sprinkles them onto the floor.

LOVEDAY: I feared that might be your reaction. Which is why I took the trouble of making some copies.

LOVEDAY produces a ream of similar documents from his briefcase.

JENNINGS: (*Nobly.*) Spare me your lies, Colonel! I'll not sign any confession. Tighten the straps! Bring back the electrodes! Do your worst – you and your minions. I'd sooner die here – forgotten and alone – shackled to a bed in this godforsaken dungeon than I would place one letter of my name on that page! I may be at your mercy – you and all the rest. Pick from me what little you can scavenge! But there is one thing you will never take. You tell me I have a bomb instead of a heart. Then inside that bomb rests the soul of an honourable man! Unleash your hellhounds, raise welts on my willing flesh! Do what wickedness you will, for you will never, ever pluck that honour from my breast and I will not sign.

LOVEDAY: Beautifully phrased. (*Looking at his watch.*) But sadly there are only twenty-four minutes to go.

JENNINGS: How dare you blackmail me!

LOVEDAY: One hates to keep a lady waiting.

JENNINGS is in turmoil.

JENNINGS: You'll let Sylvie in?

LOVEDAY: Of course.

JENNINGS: On her own?

LOVEDAY: You will be blissfully *à deux*.

Pause. JENNINGS considers tactics.

JENNINGS: Put it in writing.

LOVEDAY: I give you my word.

JENNINGS: Write it down.

LOVEDAY: As you wish.

LOVEDAY writes on a piece of paper.

JENNINGS: (*Imperiously.*) Sign it.

LOVEDAY signs.

JENNINGS snatches the paper from him and slips it inside his robe.

LOVEDAY puts his pen in JENNINGS' hand and holds the paper.

LOVEDAY: (*Pointing.*) Right there, if you will.

JENNINGS trembles.

Let me help you...

LOVEDAY tries to guide the pen.

A battle is raging inside JENNINGS. Finally...

JENNINGS: NO!

He throws the pen down.

LOVEDAY: Mr Jennings!

JENNINGS: I can't!

LOVEDAY: You must!

JENNINGS: I won't! I will not sign it.

LOVEDAY: Consider your actions very carefully –

JENNINGS: (*Shouting.*) I LOVE YOU SYLVIE!

LOVEDAY: She can't hear you –

JENNINGS: I LOVE YOU!

LOVEDAY: (*Picking up the pen.*) Come along now –

JENNINGS: Why don't *you* sign it? It hardly matters. You'll say I signed it in any case!

LOVEDAY: That's not the point.

JENNINGS: What is the point?

LOVEDAY: That would be highly unethical.

JENNINGS: You hypocrite!

LOVEDAY: We have a way of doing things on this side of the pond.

JENNINGS: (*Calling out.*) SYLVIE!

LOVEDAY: How long have you been married, Mr Jennings?

JENNINGS: What do you care?

LOVEDAY: (*Candidly.*) I'm married myself.

Pause.

JENNINGS: Twelve years.

LOVEDAY: Happily?

JENNINGS: Yes.

LOVEDAY: No hitches?

JENNINGS: Never.

LOVEDAY: Two boys?

JENNINGS: Yes.

LOVEDAY: And you still love her, after all these years?

JENNINGS: Of course –

LOVEDAY: She loves you?

JENNINGS: Yes.

LOVEDAY: Very much?

JENNINGS: What's this got to do with anything?

LOVEDAY: Think how you would feel after those twelve blissful years, if you found out she chose not to say goodbye. Before she went.

JENNINGS: (*With conviction.*) Sylvie would want me to do the honourable thing.

Beat.

LOVEDAY: The 'honourable' thing?

JENNINGS: Yes, the *honourable thing*!

LOVEDAY: Well, it's interesting you should say that.

LOVEDAY slides the confession back into his briefcase. From a side compartment he pulls out a large packet of photographs.

Would she consider that to be the honourable thing, do you think?

He passes the first photograph to JENNINGS.

JENNINGS turns ashen.

JENNINGS: (*A whisper.*) Dear God…

LOVEDAY: Or that one, maybe?

He passes on the next.

JENNINGS can't believe what he's seeing.

Enthusiastic girl, Agent Davids.

JENNINGS: This is outrageous!

LOVEDAY: Used to be a gymnast, you know. Agile as a fawn. Oh, look at that one…

JENNINGS: You have no right – this is disgusting!

LOVEDAY: I quite agree. I find the whole business utterly distasteful. But she is remarkable…

LOVEDAY is handing on a steady stream of pictures.

JENNINGS: You have no right whatsoever – (*Breaking off, seeing another one.*) Oh no…

LOVEDAY: (*Helpfully.*) The other way…

JENNINGS turns the picture round.

JENNINGS: Oh God…

LOVEDAY hands him the next.

I was asleep...she drugged me!

There are hundreds of them.

You have to destroy these!

LOVEDAY: She is pretty, though, isn't she?

JENNINGS: She'll kill me...

LOVEDAY: Almost did by the looks of it. (*With curiosity.*) Isn't that uncomfortable?

JENNINGS: Sylvie...oh God...no...

LOVEDAY: Nothing very honourable about that one, I'm afraid.

He hands it on like a used condom.

JENNINGS: (*Dizzy with horror.*) What do you want?

LOVEDAY: Talk about a square peg in a round hole.

JENNINGS: What do you want from me?

LOVEDAY: (*Of the next.*) I thought this one might be nice for the Members' Board at Lords.

JENNINGS: NO!

LOVEDAY: What will your boys make of it? Eye-opener for them, I'd imagine.

JENNINGS: You have to destroy them!

LOVEDAY: Waste them? No! I'd thought about a website.

JENNINGS: You wouldn't!

LOVEDAY: www.iseeaqc.com

JENNINGS: PLEASE!

LOVEDAY: (*Pleased.*) Come to think of it, that's rather good.

JENNINGS: I'LL DO WHATEVER YOU WANT! NO MORE!

LOVEDAY: (*With glee.*) Oh, look – this one's my favourite...

JENNINGS: I'LL SIGN!

Silence.

LOVEDAY: I beg your pardon?

JENNINGS: (*Broken.*) Destroy these photographs and I'll sign the confession.

LOVEDAY: I don't want to you to feel under any pressure.

JENNINGS: The negatives – you must destroy the negatives! All of them! You must swear –

LOVEDAY: You have my word of honour.

JENNINGS: I can't bear the thought… I… I don't want my boys growing up thinking… (*He breaks off, lost in shame.*)

LOVEDAY: (*Compassionately.*) I understand.

LOVEDAY hands him the paper and pen.

JENNINGS pauses. Then signs.

Good chap.

LOVEDAY slots the document and photographs neatly back into his briefcase.

I'll send your wife in.

JENNINGS: I don't think I can face her…

LOVEDAY: Of course you can!

JENNINGS: You will destroy them?

LOVEDAY: (*Chirpily.*) Keep your pecker up and she'll never suspect a thing.

JENNINGS: (*Looking at the clock.*) There's only nineteen minutes to go…

LOVEDAY: No need to worry. (*Indicating the walls.*) There's eight feet of reinforced concrete. We'll be quite safe.

LOVEDAY goes for the door. A thought…

Bonne chance!

LOVEDAY exits.

The moment he's gone, panic sets it.

JENNINGS struggles to free himself from his shackles. He pulls with all his might. Failing, he grips the frame of the bed with his hands and begins desperately kicking his legs, attempting to free them.

SYLVIE enters silently. She wears a visitor's badge. She watches her husband for a few moments in silence as he struggles.

His behaviour smacks of lunacy.

SYLVIE: (*Softly.*) Charles?

JENNINGS stops abruptly and turns to face her.

(*At the sight of him.*) Dear God.

JENNINGS: Oh, Sylvie! Sylvie!

She takes in the austere surroundings.

They told me I couldn't see you. They tried to blackmail me, my darling – my sweet –

He holds out his arms.

SYLVIE: (*With tenderness and pity.*) Oh, Charles…

JENNINGS: Are you alright?

SYLVIE: Aren't you cold? It's so dark down here –

JENNINGS: You have to help me!

SYLVIE: I came as soon as I heard.

JENNINGS: You can't imagine what the last hour's been like! I've been insulted, threatened, humiliated – I don't know where I am or what I'm doing here or if the outside world even knows I'm in this godforsaken pit at all! I've been tortured – abused! I didn't think it was possible to treat someone as I have been treated! They're inhuman! They're mad!

SYLVIE: Try and keep calm. Everyone's doing their best to help you. This isn't easy for any of us.

JENNINGS: (*Tenderly.*) You look wonderful.

SYLVIE: You look awful.

JENNINGS: I've been electrocuted!

SYLVIE: Probably just treatment.

JENNINGS: It's not treatment! It's torture! This isn't a hospital, darling, it's a torture chamber! Those clamps you use to start a car with – they attached them to my legs – they electrocuted me! Now I need you to listen to me very carefully –

SYLVIE: You only have to ask.

JENNINGS: How much have they told you?

SYLVIE: Have there been developments?

JENNINGS: What did they tell you? Exactly. You must tell me. Quickly.

SYLVIE: They said it didn't go well. They told me to come immediately.

JENNINGS: That's all? Nothing else?

SYLVIE: No.

JENNINGS: Nothing at all?

SYLVIE: Why? What is it?

Pause.

JENNINGS: (*Whispered.*) You have to get me out of here.

SYLVIE: Why are you whispering?

JENNINGS tugs on his ear to indicate that they are listening.

Who's listening?

He points to the walls.

JENNINGS: (*Coughing to disguise the sound.*) Where are we?

SYLVIE: Hm?

JENNINGS: (*Mouthed.*) Where are we?

SYLVIE: (*Getting it.*) Oh! 'Where are we?'

    JENNINGS shushes her but nods vigorously.

    I can't tell you.

JENNINGS: What!

SYLVIE: I promised I wouldn't.

JENNINGS: For goodness' sake!

SYLVIE: They told me specifically –

JENNINGS: (*Whispered.*) You've got to get me out of here!

SYLVIE: It's for your own good. You're not well. They're very concerned for you.

JENNINGS: This isn't a hospital! It's some sort of prison!

SYLVIE: It's not a prison. They call it a facility.

JENNINGS: You have to help me escape!

SYLVIE: Try to be calm. You have the top men in their field looking after you.

JENNINGS: They're insane! They want to get rid of me!

SYLVIE: That's not a very nice thing to say. Mr Gibbons has tried very hard to give you –

JENNINGS: Doctor Gibbons is shortly to be struck off!

SYLVIE: (*Patiently.*) Mr Gibbons has tried very hard to give you the best possible care. I happen to know that he's doing his best to ensure that when the time comes –

JENNINGS: They're lying to you, Sylvie! They lie to everyone!

SYLVIE: What do you want me to do about it?

JENNINGS: (*Whispered.*) Help me escape! Get me out of here!

SYLVIE: What? Blast a hole in the wall?

JENNINGS: There must be a way!

SYLVIE: And what would happen even if you did escape? What good would that do us?

JENNINGS: What good would it do? Sylvie, I need to get out of here! I want to live again! With you! In our house! With our children! Like normal people! Like it was before! I want to forget this ever happened. Don't you see? Nobody's listening to me… You're my last chance! If you don't help me I might die here!

SYLVIE: You see, this is exactly what I've been talking about.

JENNINGS: I might die, Sylvie! Do you hear me?

SYLVIE: You're not being realistic.

JENNINGS: I'm being utterly realistic –

SYLVIE: You've just come out of a very serious operation. You can't expect to be back on your feet straight away.

JENNINGS: 'On my feet'? They've strapped me to the bed!

SYLVIE: And even if they hadn't, it wouldn't change the fact that – whatever you say now and whether you escape or not – you're going to go bang very shortly.

JENNINGS reels.

You can't go on persuading yourself that you might die here when it's already certain that you will. This has been the pattern all our married life, Charles. You set unattainable goals for yourself.

JENNINGS' life is falling apart before his eyes.

I don't want you to think I don't understand. I do. It must be dreadful for you too. But in situations like this, it's always harder for the ones left behind. I know that your thoughts are for me now, which is why I married you in the first place

– for exactly that sweet selflessness. You wouldn't want me
to give up. You'd want me to get on with my life. I've been
lucky. I've done the grieving process early and I know full
well it's not going to make you any happier to see me cry
now. We've had some wonderful times together. But I've
asked myself some important questions recently. Not just
about you – or us, but about…life. And the conclusion I've
come to – and it's brought me solace – is that, when you
think about it, life's really no more than a weekend break
in a two star hotel. At some point, you have to settle up. It's
the one thing we can be sure of and there's reassurance in
that. It's not lonely there. In fact, Death's a very fashionable
destination. We're all going eventually. It just so happens
you're booked on the two o'clock sleeper. I will join you, but
on a later train. That's all.

The conclusiveness of the philosophy leaves JENNINGS catatonic.
They stare at each other for a long time in silence.

JENNINGS: (*Weakly.*) Sylvie…

SYLVIE: I take it you've left instructions for the disposal of…
whatever's left…after the blast?

JENNINGS: (*Dazed.*) Hm?

SYLVIE: I do wish you'd think about these things –

JENNINGS: You know it goes off in fourteen minutes?

SYLVIE: Yes. Paul told me this morning.

Pause.

JENNINGS: (*Politely, tinged with misery.*) Who is Paul?

SYLVIE: Mr Gibbons. He's been very good to us. He wanted to
give me time to get used to the idea of losing you.

JENNINGS: He told you this morning?

SYLVIE: Apparently it's all been pretty hush hush.

JENNINGS: And you're already used to the idea that I'm gone?

SYLVIE: You know how practical I am.

JENNINGS: But what if I don't?

SYLVIE: Don't what?

JENNINGS: (*Not wanting to say it.*) You know…

SYLVIE: This is what I'm saying about being realistic. Right now you have to face the inescapable fact that the thing inside you is going to explode in fourteen minutes –

JENNINGS: (*Looking at his clock.*) Thirteen!

SYLVIE: (*Pragmatically.*) There's no point spending your last few minutes arguing about whether or not it's going to happen.

JENNINGS: Talk to them, Sylvie! There must be something they can do! YOU HAVE TO HELP ME!

SYLVIE: You're not in the courtroom now –

JENNINGS: This is jungle law! We are outside justice. What you do in the next sixty seconds may decide whether I live or die. You have to do something! QUICKLY!

SYLVIE: It's always a last minute panic with you –

JENNINGS: I want to see our children grow up! I want to be a good father to them!

SYLVIE: You've a funny way of showing it.

JENNINGS: Listen to me, Sylvie! What if it doesn't go off? What if the whole thing's been a mistake, or there's a malfunction, or the fuse goes wrong, or it's a very little explosion and I can hold it in? What if it's all been a lie in the first place? Hm? What then? What happens if I don't go? Think about what you're saying! You'll regret it for the rest of our life!

SYLVIE: (*Horrified.*) Our life?

JENNINGS: I'm going to pull through this! Don't ask me how I know – it's an instinct! A gut feeling! You'll see! But right now I need you!

SYLVIE: I'm afraid that's not going to wash.

JENNINGS: I'm frightened, Sylvie!

SYLVIE: Besides, I have to consider Paul.

JENNINGS: Paul!?

SYLVIE: Yes. Paul.

JENNINGS: What's Paul got to do with this?

SYLVIE: Mr Gibbons is very sensitive.

JENNINGS: What about me?

SYLVIE: You've got skin like an elephant, Charles. Paul has an artistic temperament.

JENNINGS: Bugger Paul!

SYLVIE: Don't be coarse.

JENNINGS: You know what I think?

SYLVIE: Paul has been very concerned all along –

JENNINGS: If it wasn't for Paul –

SYLVIE: (*An outburst.*) YOU HAD IT INSTALLED IN THE FIRST PLACE!

Silence.

JENNINGS: What did you say?

SYLVIE: Well? Didn't you?

JENNINGS: NO! I did not have it 'installed'!

SYLVIE: You're completely blameless.

JENNINGS: Sylvie, for God's sake – it's ME!

SYLVIE: That's supposed to make it easier?

JENNINGS: Look at me!

SYLVIE: Bombs don't get there by themselves.

JENNINGS: One minute I'm in the hospital, waiting for an operation, the next I'm down here, locked in a cell with…

(*He looks at the alarm clock.*) – nine minutes to go! I can say, hand on my heart –

SYLVIE: You don't have a heart.

JENNINGS: LET ME FINISH! I can say, with nine minutes to go, honestly and truthfully: I don't how this happened! They took me from the hospital and they brought me here –

SYLVIE: *You* brought us here!

JENNINGS: They kidnapped me!

SYLVIE: Thank God they did!

JENNINGS: We have nine minutes! Whatever they've said to you –

SYLVIE: I told them at the time I was worried. Not that I seriously thought you'd go through with it. But I suppose that's the nature of extremism.

Pause.

JENNINGS: (*Clear as a bell.*) Sylvie, did you have anything to do with this?

SYLVIE: All I did was tell Paul the situation.

JENNINGS: What situation?

SYLVIE: I was very concerned. I had no one else to turn to.

JENNINGS: (*Time is running out.*) What situation?

SYLVIE: All the horrible things you'd been saying. If you'd said them about me, I could have put up with it. As it was, I had to bite my tongue.

JENNINGS: Sylvie, this is a matter of my life and death: what things was I saying?

SYLVIE: I thought you might do something stupid. I felt very uncomfortable.

JENNINGS: WHAT THINGS?

SYLVIE: 'Bloody this' and 'bloody that'! I'd never heard you use such language. It was very violent. 'The government had no right' and 'who do they think they are?' And all that when they're doing their best to protect us. Everyone knows we're under attack. It isn't just ungrateful. It struck me as…well, dangerous.

JENNINGS: That was a conversation –

SYLVIE: Conversation is talking, Charles. You kept going on and on about the need to do something. 'Something has to be done!' You kept saying it. You went on and on about it. Like a fanatic. I didn't know what you were planning. And if it happened to be something violent – as it has turned out to be – I could have been implicated. Where would that have left the children? When Paul mentioned I could come in and give a statement, it sounded sensible.

JENNINGS: Statement?

SYLVIE: I could have been arrested.

JENNINGS: When? When did you do this, Sylvie?

SYLVIE: Oh – months ago. I can't remember.

JENNINGS: (*To himself.*) Tip-off… Psmith said there was a tip-off…

SYLVIE: Paul was very understanding.

JENNINGS: You said you met him this morning –

SYLVIE: He told me about the bomb this morning. I've known Paul going on a year.

JENNINGS: Wait a minute –

SYLVIE: You don't have a minute, Charles.

JENNINGS: You went to the police –

SYLVIE: (*Clarifying.*) With Paul.

JENNINGS: – and told them that a practising member of the Bar – your husband, incidentally – with two small children, was planning to give up his life and his career to wage jihad?

89

SYLVIE: (*Qualifying that.*) I told them I was worried.

JENNINGS: And I suppose Paul –

SYLVIE: Don't go blaming Paul when he's the one who risked his life to save you!

JENNINGS: He didn't risk anything!

SYLVIE: He didn't have to sew you up! (*With emotional gusto.*) You're bloody ungrateful sometimes!

She is on the verge of tears. There is something in her expression that JENNINGS picks up. She won't look at him.

JENNINGS: Sylvie…

SYLVIE: Paul is an extraordinary man! He's been through an awful lot on your account and I won't have you saying things against him! (*With real emotion.*) I won't! I simply won't!

Pause.

It just happened. I didn't plan it this way.

JENNINGS picks up the alarm clock.

JENNINGS: I have six minutes to live.

SYLVIE: I think you'd like him if you got to know him.

Pause.

JENNINGS: I want to say this – while there's still time: I love you. I don't pretend to understand why you've done what you've done. But if I die here, I die knowing that you are the one woman I have ever truly loved. And you can stop this. There is still time.

GIBBONS: (*Over the intercom.*) What about Nurse Davids?

The mood is broken.

SYLVIE: What about her, Charles?

JENNINGS: Gibbons?

SYLVIE: What was it? A last stand?

JENNINGS: Sylvie, listen to me –

SYLVIE: You see this badge? It says 'Mrs Jennings'. You know how that makes me feel?

JENNINGS: They're lying to you –

SYLVIE: Come off it, Charles. The photographs are pinned up in the corridor. They point at them as they go past.

JENNINGS: I was drugged, Sylvie – I wasn't even conscious!

SYLVIE: You know how cheap that makes me feel?

JENNINGS: It's the truth!

SYLVIE: What? You were date-raped on the NHS?

JENNINGS: She's not a nurse! She's an agent! She won't even remember!

NURSE DAVIDS: (*On intercom.*) It was quite good actually.

JENNINGS: I was asleep! My eyes are closed! Look for yourself –

SYLVIE: You never looked at me. Not once. In all our married life.

JENNINGS: Sylvie – this isn't the time! Talk to Gibbons! He's the only one who can stop this!

JENNINGS suddenly shudders and turns pale.

I can feel it…

SYLVIE: What?

JENNINGS: It's starting…

GIBBONS: (*On intercom.*) Five minutes and counting.

JENNINGS: It's happening…

GIBBONS: (*On intercom.*) You'll have to come out now, Angel.

SYLVIE: I have to go, Charles.

JENNINGS: (*Appealing to her.*) Don't leave me…

SYLVIE: I've no intention of diminishing your glory by sharing it.

She's at the door.

JENNINGS: Wait! Tell me one thing – tell me honestly… (*Summoning all his courage.*) Did you ever love me?

SYLVIE: Ever?

JENNINGS: Yes.

Pause.

SYLVIE: Love's a hard thing to define.

JENNINGS: (*With infinite sorrow.*) Say goodbye to the boys. (*His throat tightening.*) Don't let them cry. Not too much. Tell them I love them. Tell them…Daddy tried his best. Maybe one day they'll understand.

SYLVIE: I'll tell them.

JENNINGS: You will take care of them?

SYLVIE: Paul and I plan to do a lot of travelling. The reward money's given us a cushion.

JENNINGS: (*Sensing disaster.*) Sylvie…

SYLVIE: Put yourself in the boys' shoes. There's a scandal when the junior girls wear headscarves. Just imagine what the playground will be like at break-time when it turns out their daddy was a failed suicide bomber. And frankly Paul doesn't want the responsibility. At least in a foster home they'll have some chance of a normal life.

GIBBONS: (*On intercom.*) Three minutes.

The faint sound of a warning siren.

SYLVIE: I have to go.

She kisses him on the cheek.

Goodbye.

She exits.

JENNINGS is left totally alone. His eyes are empty pools.

A succession of doors thunder closed (off). Only the distant siren intrudes into the moment.

A breath.

Then the first shudders.

He cannot hold back the tide…

JENNINGS weeps and weeps and he cannot stop.

JENNINGS: SYLVIE!

His howl echoes in the chamber.

Sylvie…

Silence.

Straining over, he raises up the alarm clock from the table. He watches helplessly as the hands circle the face.

A barely audible ticking begins.

JENNINGS has one last, desperate attempt to free himself. It is a sorry sight.

A viewing gallery appears above JENNINGS' bed, hitherto unseen.

An intercom communicates with the chamber below.

PSMITH enters the gallery.

AGENT PSMITH: (*On intercom.*) You there, Jezeera?

JENNINGS: Get it over with! Do it! For God's sake – do it!

AGENT PSMITH: We picked up that Jones fella. You were right – massive laundering operation. In the course of the raid they arrested a number of women and confiscated several hundred kilos of white powder.

JENNINGS: (*To himself, in despair.*) Bloody, bloody fool…

AGENT PSMITH: (*Not hearing.*) What's that?

JENNINGS: His brother runs a Laundromat!

AGENT PSMITH: (*Intercom, not understanding.*) Right. Better pick him up as well. Thanks for the lead. Safe trip, Jezeera. Oh, Agent Davids wants to say a few words…

NURSE DAVIDS enters the gallery.

In the background the sounds of a party can be heard.

She is clutching a champagne flute.

NURSE DAVIDS: (*Intercom.*) I wanted to say goodbye… (*In the background someone says 'Charles'.*) – Charles…and thank you…I had a smashing time. I hope someday you'll find it in your heart to forgive me… (*She giggles.*) Actually, that's quite funny…

SYLVIE enters and takes the microphone from NURSE DAVIDS.

SYLVIE: (*Intercom.*) Oh, I forgot to say, Charles. Flowers. For the funeral. A decision has to be made. I thought lilies.

JENNINGS stays silent, his gaze thousands of miles away.

GIBBONS enters the gallery.

Charles? Can you hear me? Charles…? (*Then off the microphone, muted.*) Is there something wrong with this thing?

GIBBONS: (*Taking over the microphone, protective.*) You might at least show some courtesy to your wife!

JENNINGS: Take care of her.

GIBBONS: (*Confidential, man to man.*) She's fretting about these flowers. You know how she gets.

JENNINGS is flooded with memories.

JENNINGS: Roses…

GIBBONS: What's that?

JENNINGS: Roses.

GIBBONS: Yes. Well. No hard feelings, eh.

Silence descends. A moment.

(*Intercom, an afterthought.*) Oh, and on a practical note, the brace position will probably be quickest.

JENNINGS looks to heaven.

LOVEDAY enters the gallery.

LOVEDAY: (*Intercom.*) Jennings! Loveday here. Glad I caught you. The Home Secretary has asked me to send his condolences and to tell you personally, in the nicest possible way, that he hopes it hurts. (*Beat.*) It's the attention to detail I admire. (*As an afterthought.*) Any last words?

JENNINGS stares out impassively. Then from somewhere…

JENNINGS: Stop the madness.

Pause.

LOVEDAY: Yes. Yes, that's rather good.

But the mood is somehow sobered.

Better sign off now. Good show.

A final 'Cheers!' and the gallery goes black.

JENNINGS: (*A thought striking him.*) There's no chance this thing might…misfire…when the time comes?

Silence.

JENNINGS is once again alone in the gloom. JENNINGS' chest begins to beat. Mesmerised, JENNINGS watches the second hand circle the face of his clock.

The distant ticking of the clock gets closer and closer, growing in volume until it fills the room like a roar.

JENNINGS holds the clock tight to his chest and braces.

Lights fade slowly to black as the ticking builds to a climax…

Then suddenly stops.

Lights up again.

JENNINGS has his eyes screwed tight shut, still braced for the explosion. Slowly he peels open his eyes and looks in disbelief at the clock face. His look of terror changes to one of sheer, joyful disbelief.

(*Quietly.*) I'm alive…I'm alive…

MR JENNINGS laughs the maniacal laugh of a man reprieved from a death sentence. The vast panoply of life unfolds before him in an instant.

I'M ALIVE! FUCK YOU! IT HASN'T WORKED! FUCK YOU ALL! NOW WHO'S GOT THE LAST LAUGH! NOW WE'LL SEE WHO'S RESPONSIBLE!

He continues his rabid joy for exactly one minute.

Blackout.

And a massive explosion.

The End.